First World War
and Army of Occupation
War Diary
France, Belgium and Germany

47 DIVISION
Headquarters, Branches and Services
Royal Army Ordnance Corps
Deputy Assistant Director Ordnance Services
16 March 1915 - 28 February 1919

WO95/2716/1

The Naval & Military Press Ltd
www.nmarchive.com
Published in association with The National Archives

Published by

The Naval & Military Press Ltd

Unit 10 Ridgewood Industrial Park,

Uckfield, East Sussex,

TN22 5QE England

Tel: +44 (0) 1825 749494

www.naval-military-press.com

www.nmarchive.com

This diary has been reprinted in facsimile from the original. Any imperfections are inevitably reproduced and the quality may fall short of modern type and cartographic standards.

© Crown Copyright
Images reproduced by permission of The National Archives, London, England, 2015.

Contents

Document type	Place/Title	Date From	Date To
Heading	WO95/2716/1		
Heading	47th Division D.A. Dir. Ordnance Services Mar 1915-Feb 1919		
Heading	War Diary of D.A.D.O.S. 2nd London Division from 16th March to 31st March 1915. Vol I.		
War Diary	Boulogne	16/03/1915	17/03/1915
War Diary	Aire	18/03/1915	19/03/1915
War Diary	Marles	20/03/1915	30/03/1915
Heading	D.A.D.O.S. 2nd London Division Vol II. 1-30.4.15.		
War Diary	Marles.	01/04/1915	16/04/1915
War Diary	Mensecq.	17/04/1915	23/04/1915
War Diary	Bethune	24/04/1915	30/04/1915
Heading	47th Division D.A.D.O.S. 47th Division Vol III May to June 1915.		
Heading	War Diary of D.A.D.O.S. 47th Division From 1-5-15. To 30-6-15.		
War Diary	Bethune	01/05/1915	02/06/1915
War Diary	Verquin.	03/06/1915	11/06/1915
War Diary	Noeux-Les-Mines.	12/06/1915	30/06/1915
Heading	47th Division D.A.D.O.S. 47th Division Vol IV.		
Heading	War Diary of D.A.D.O.S. 47th Division (Major J.H. Buckland) A.O.D. From:- 1-7-15. To:- 31-7-15.		
War Diary	Noeux-Les-Mines.	01/07/1915	31/07/1915
Heading	47th Division D.A.D.O.S. 47th Division Vol V. Aug No. 1.15.		
Heading	War Diary of D.A.D.O.S. 47th Division (Major Buckland A.O.D.) From:- 1.8.15. To:- 31.8.16.		
War Diary	Noeux-Les-Mines.	01/08/1915	01/08/1915
War Diary	Gosuay	01/08/1915	01/08/1915
War Diary	Noeux-Les-Mines.	02/08/1915	03/08/1915
War Diary	Gosuay	04/08/1915	31/08/1915
Heading	47th Division D.A.D.O.S. 47th Division Vol VI. Sept. 15.		
Heading	War Diary of D.A.D.O.S. 47th Division (Major Buckland A.O.D.) 1-9-15 to 30-9-15.		
War Diary	Gosuay	01/09/1915	03/09/1915
War Diary	Drouvin	04/09/1915	25/09/1915
War Diary	Noeux-Les-Mines.	26/09/1915	30/09/1915
War Diary	Gosuay	30/09/1915	30/09/1915
Heading	D.A.D.O.S. 47th Divn. Oct 15 Vol VII. 121/7493		
War Diary	Gosuay	01/10/1915	05/10/1915
War Diary	Noeux-Les-Mines.	05/10/1915	14/10/1915
War Diary	Mazingarbe	15/10/1915	31/10/1915
Heading	D.A.D.O.S. 47th Div. Nov. 1915 Vol VIII 121/7637.		
War Diary	Mazingarbe	01/11/1915	14/11/1915
War Diary	Marles-Les-Mines	15/11/1915	17/11/1915
War Diary	Marles	18/11/1915	18/11/1915
War Diary	Marles-Les-Mines.	19/11/1915	25/11/1915
War Diary	Noeux-Les-Mines.	26/11/1915	27/11/1915
War Diary	Marles-Les-Mines.	28/11/1915	30/11/1915

Heading	D.A.D.O.S. 47th Div. Dec. Vol IX.		
War Diary	Marles-Les-Mines.	01/12/1915	15/12/1915
War Diary	Noeux-Les-Mines.	15/12/1915	16/12/1915
War Diary	Marles-Les-Mines.	17/12/1916	31/12/1916
Heading	D.A.D.O.S. 47 Div Jan Vol X.		
War Diary	Noeux-Les-Mines.	01/01/1916	31/01/1916
Heading	War Diary Capt. A.J. Shead D.A.D.O.S. 47th Division From February 1st-29th 1916. Vol XI.		
War Diary	Noeux-Les-Mines.	01/02/1916	16/02/1916
War Diary	Lilliers	28/02/1916	28/02/1916
Heading	D.A.D. O.S. 47 Div Vol XII.		
War Diary	Lillers	01/03/1916	01/03/1916
War Diary	Bruay	09/03/1916	15/03/1916
War Diary	Menil Bonches	16/03/1916	17/03/1916
War Diary	Fremicourt	20/03/1916	31/03/1916
Heading	D.A.D.O.S. 47 Div Vol XIII.		
War Diary	Fresnicourt	01/04/1916	26/05/1916
War Diary	Bruay	27/05/1916	13/06/1916
War Diary	Barlin	14/06/1916	17/07/1916
War Diary	Camblain L'Abbe	18/07/1916	30/07/1916
War Diary	Flers	01/08/1916	15/08/1916
War Diary	Frohen-Le-Grand	04/08/1916	04/08/1916
War Diary	Yvrench	06/08/1916	15/08/1916
War Diary	St Riquier	15/08/1916	20/08/1916
War Diary	Vignacourt	22/08/1916	22/08/1916
War Diary	Freshencourt	25/08/1916	10/09/1916
War Diary	Albert.	11/09/1916	22/09/1916
War Diary	Albert	20/09/1916	20/09/1916
War Diary	Albert	03/10/1916	03/10/1916
War Diary	Fricourt	08/10/1916	10/10/1916
War Diary	Albert	14/10/1916	14/10/1916
War Diary	L'Etoile	15/10/1916	16/10/1916
War Diary	Reninghelst	16/10/1916	16/05/1917
War Diary	Ouderdom	16/05/1917	31/05/1917
War Diary	Ouderdom G.23.c.9.4.	03/06/1917	11/06/1917
War Diary	Westoutre	13/06/1917	25/07/1917
War Diary	Berthen. R.21.d.5.2.	25/07/1917	28/07/1917
War Diary	Berthen	28/07/1917	06/08/1917
War Diary	Wizernes	10/08/1917	17/08/1917
War Diary	28.G.14.d.c.	18/08/1917	21/08/1917
War Diary	Oudendom	21/08/1917	19/09/1917
War Diary	Godewaersvelde	21/09/1917	23/09/1917
War Diary	St Catherine	24/09/1917	30/11/1917
War Diary	Neuville	01/12/1917	05/12/1917
War Diary	Ytres	06/12/1917	16/12/1917
War Diary	Heilly	20/12/1917	05/01/1918
War Diary	Etricourt	06/01/1918	23/01/1918
War Diary	Little Wood Camp Ytres	23/01/1918	22/02/1918
War Diary	Bus.	23/02/1918	21/03/1918
War Diary	Combles	22/03/1918	23/03/1918
War Diary	Albert	23/03/1918	23/03/1918
War Diary	Albert-Amiens Rd Nr Ribemont	24/03/1918	24/03/1918
War Diary	Warloy	25/03/1918	25/03/1918
War Diary	Vauchelles	26/03/1918	26/03/1918
War Diary	Puchvillers	27/03/1918	27/03/1918
War Diary	Rubempre	29/03/1918	08/04/1918

War Diary	Domart	12/04/1918	12/04/1918
War Diary	Canchy	13/04/1918	01/05/1918
War Diary	Beaucourt	02/05/1918	18/06/1918
War Diary	Cavillon	20/06/1918	25/07/1918
War Diary	Molliens-Au-Bois	01/08/1918	09/08/1918
War Diary	Pont Noyelles.	12/08/1918	25/08/1918
War Diary	Heilly	26/08/1918	26/08/1918
War Diary	Hidden Wood Mametz	30/08/1918	04/09/1918
War Diary	Maurepas	05/09/1918	05/09/1918
War Diary	Allouagne	09/09/1918	21/09/1918
War Diary	Hautecloque	27/09/1918	27/09/1918
War Diary	Willems	01/11/1918	01/11/1918
War Diary	La Tombe	12/11/1918	12/11/1918
War Diary	Chereng	17/11/1918	17/11/1918
War Diary	Loninghem	26/11/1918	26/11/1918
War Diary	Allouagne	28/11/1918	26/12/1918
War Diary	Auchel	01/01/1919	19/02/1919
War Diary	Pernes	25/02/1919	28/02/1919

WO 95/22161

47TH DIVISION

D.A.DIR. ORDNANCE SERVICES

MAR 1915-FEB 1919

47TH DIVISION

Confidential

War Diary
of
D.A.D.O.S.
2nd London Division

from 16th March to 31st March. 1915.

Vol I.

O.Co.S.

137/4885.

Mar 15
Feb 19

Army Form C. 2118.

WAR DIARY
or
INTELLIGENCE SUMMARY.
(Erase heading not required.)

Instructions regarding War Diaries and Intelligence Summaries are contained in F.S. Regs., Part II. and the Staff Manual respectively. Title pages will be prepared in manuscript.

Hour, Date, Place	Summary of Events and Information	Remarks and references to Appendices
BOULOGNE 16 March	Landed from England via FOLKESTONE with ADS HofOpr Personnel. 2nd London Divn. T.F.	
do 17th	Reported to Base Commandant who wired G.H.Q. for instructions. Wire received from G.H.Q. to report to Hd Qrs 1st Army ATRE.	
ATRE 18th	Proceeded by supply train that night. Arrived 6 a.m. Reported HdQrs 1st Army. Interviewed by D.D.S. Instructed to get in touch with DOO's of 1st or 2nd	
19th	Divns. to learn system.	
Merville 20th	Proceeded by motor to Merville to Merv – HdQr 2 Lon Divn. In touch with DOO 1st Divn.	
21st	do Received orders from G.S.O.	
	to arrange & claim to base of Fur waistcoat drawn by 3rd London Infy Bde.	
22nd	Routine. Posthood etc. Ordered 1200 rifle covers by order of S.S.O.	
24th } 25th }	Furwaistcoats returned to RTO CHOCQUES S. No Eqpce G.R. Orders yet received. Visited DOOS 1st Army. Kattan. No office yet available.	

WAR DIARY
or
INTELLIGENCE SUMMARY.
(Erase heading not required.)

Army Form C. 2118.

Hour, Date, Place	Summary of Events and Information	Remarks and references to Appendices
MAR 1918. 29th. 30.	Circular letter received re various replies of in clearing for Bulk items - 48 lyddite shell 4.7 Q.F. received to complete equipment of Heavy Battery. Drivers & amn day to Battery at BETHUNE on way to N° 1 group Heavy Artillery Bde. Capt. J. Schools G. Riordan revived. Daily routine carried out. Railhead visited & stores reviewed & distributed. Petitioning parties R.V.D. visited. Ordinary work of minimum carried out. Thus latter up heavy. Units do not appear to have returned back all their deficiencies prior to embarkation. to some cases have lost parts of their equipment on afterwards when taken over 9 R.G.A. 20 where we enemy.	[signature] Lieut. Col? D.A.D.O.S. 2 don Div. T.E.

12/5/111

DADOS 2nd London Division

Vol II 1 – 30.4.15.

WAR DIARY or INTELLIGENCE SUMMARY

Army Form C. 2118.

Hour, Date, Place	Summary of Events and Information	Remarks and references to Appendices
NAPLES. 1st April	20 G.S. wagon burnt out, received from Base. Buried to put train — hay wagons — Divisional laundry started. Reinforcing drafts — 191 men in all — arrived from Base depôt — uniform shortage in provision of blankets — reported to A.A.+Q.M.G.	
2nd.	Returned to Base. Consignment of gum boots, sent to England to withdraw these from G.O's already uninforcing. Other Divs who are already returning these. Visit of DDOS 4th Army.	
3rd.	Ditto. Saw all Ch MO or OMS at conference. Reported. Septics cleared up. Difficulties.	
6th.	Sgt Shoemaker reported for duty with Div Shoemakers Shop. Takeover building premises. Shop of HQ Div Only. Sewn St. Took over of snack made room 250 footballs for Divl. Festh. many to wet weather. Supplies of APO and QMG. Imposed on move of 250 tents to Base HQ for time being.	
8th.	Hay nets received. Issues commenced.	
7th.	Decided to return of warm clothing by Gsoc Div. Went to AIRE to DDOS 4th Army re R.F. blankets + vein of warm clothing.	

WAR DIARY
or
INTELLIGENCE SUMMARY.

(Erase heading not required.)

Army Form C. 2118.

Hour, Date, Place	Summary of Events and Information	Remarks and references to Appendices

MARLES. 8th April

D.D.S. G.H.Q. visited Railhead. Services ackg. 25 Pdr. to Telephone Eqpt. Radios 6" & 7" Box RA and S.A.A. N.922

9th —
Sent to 6 Inty Battns and 16 A.Div Artillery being attached Div Divn Amm dressed to Spun 62 R refilling point in BETHUNE. Went to BETHUNE & earmarked store.

10th
Transferred all bulk vehicles from unit attached from Divisions to Corps Handling. to disss. arrangements for Corps Ammunition to be responsible for sorting load v Handling bulk stores at REBOURNE. refilling park.

11th
Opened refilling point BETHUNE.
Saw 2/o Lou Fuels to R.E. who have returned from XXVIII Div. as vehicles outstanding indents & deficiencies sent enquiries to ammo Orgs as to return of warm clothing. Reported that Boots were now coming in for repair.

12th
Handed over surplus G.S. wagon rect is comn from Rous to 1st Corps

D.D.S. re loads to repair
Relieved rifle covers. for issue - 16 OTY 1st Corps

WAR DIARY
or
INTELLIGENCE SUMMARY.
(Erase heading not required.)

Army Form C. 2118.

Hour, Date, Place	Summary of Events and Information	Remarks and references to Appendices
MARLES. 13th	100 prs boots rec'd at Shoemakers shop for repair. Visited 17th & 18th Battns re suitability of canvas rifle covers.	
14th	Visited R.D.C.S. 1st Army re question of return of worn clothing. Also saw 5th & 8th Inf. Bde Hd Qrs and R.A. Hd Qrs on subject of Boards of Enquiry.	
15th	Saw G.R.A. re fuzes which have been opened – is an item with report required by G.H.Q. Saw L & Mfy/Bde re strain with report required by G.H.Q. Saw L & Mfy/Bde re fuzes and shrapnel T.P. reported unsuitable. H.Q. re boards of Enquiry. Parts for repair enroute in at for work in trenches. Went to E.S.S.A.R.S. re alteration to round [illegible] and 5th Amm Coll. Saw No 65 fuses.	
16th	Referred to 1st Army an Ammunition Ship CASUALTIES. Asked re fuze filled & dummy cartridge infection. Visited D.A.C.D. re hammer and 5th Amm Coll. re material for repair. Spoke to 1st M. re difficulty re reinforcements. Forwarded demands for spare parts for Cyclists. Also 1st M Cap'd rifle for C/O. Saw Battalion Armourer. Proposed for repair 15 cycle rifle clips to 1st Army.	

WAR DIARY
INTELLIGENCE SUMMARY
(Erase heading not required.)

Army Form C. 2118.

Hour, Date, Place	Summary of Events and Information	Remarks and references to Appendices
MENSECQ 17th	Hd Qrs Div moved from MARLES to MENSECQ. 10 tons stores received. This is rather more than can be conveniently handled, especially as units are at present training. Issues in sort of 1st & 2nd Div Ammo almost daily. Omission of receipt of notification of issue to battalions being cancelled caused a great deal of extra handling & work of time. A.O. stores were brought to BILLONCQUE instead of being sent to BETHUNE. Reported to A.O. D.S.S. 5000 pr boots for H.M Queen received & distributed in accordance with list given by Adjutant Genl. 5900(000) rifle ammo received from Ord 1072dpr of hy rattn. Losses roughly 2030 lbs. Stev stores delivered today to 19th Battery R.F.A. took stores. Quite right ammn for base. Continual movement of units to & from Bs & 2nd Div makes posn of personnel of A.O.D. stores v. difficult. Boards of Demand on team clothing pr return 15 PAPP 18 received from 3 Infy Bdes.	
18th		
19th	Decision of A Corps that no issues of cable exista for Batteries R.F.A. can be allowed over that allowed in G.R.O. 350	

WAR DIARY
or
INTELLIGENCE SUMMARY.

Army Form C. 2118.

(Erase heading not required.)

Hour, Date, Place	Summary of Events and Information	Remarks and references to Appendices
MENSECQ. 20th April.	Steel loops for Owen's Carriers 15 per Rifle received for 7th Bde R.F.A. Notified C.R.A. in action the labour would still actually required in accordance with L./C. 7022.	
21st.	Return of Rifle Grenadiers returned to Brigade. Ordered to supply 16 rifle S.M.L.E. of firing grenades from Bar. as well to fire from L.M. rifle. Arranged with R.S.O. to keep first bulged rifles for this purpose. Reported to Divison that Army Bde. was not up to more than 2690 rounds per gun for guns already supplied by him.	
22nd.	Made preliminary arrangements for move to BETHUNE on 23rd. Move cancelled pro tem.	
23rd.	Owing to practically all units being in BETHUNE area had many wanted officers in from ALLOUAGNE to draw their back again struggle as unable to find billets for them. Orders received for move of B.Q. of Div. 1 from Div. H.Q. Div. moved to BETHUNE. Transferred Bde. Warrant Officers	
BETHUNE 24th.	& M.T. details from ALLOUAGNE to Army for use annual of clothes from Base had to purchase locally CV 9/5 & Kilos Sent A. & Q.M.G. 2nd Div. a report on rifle grenades Report from 15th Batt. that one Lewis was abandoned owing to enemy's Report from 15th Batt. that one Lewis was abandoned owing to enemy's whiz-bang shells.	

WAR DIARY
INTELLIGENCE SUMMARY
(Erase heading not required.)

Army Form C. 2118.

Hour, Date, Place	Summary of Events and Information	Remarks and references to Appendices
BETHUNE. 25th April	Proceeded to Hd Qrs 5 Lan Inf Bde re question of rifle grenades. To see spectators in trenches at FESTUBERT. Reported 1st A Army. Squadron K.E.H. arrived to join Divl Cavalry.	
26th	Visited Squadron I.C.E.H. — Equipment practically complete. About to urgent indents for colts selected from R.A. units at YPRES. 15 See DDGS 1st Army. Important & Lucknow received verbal permission to wire Base cavalry depotage with further indents period by C.R.A. — More Munros will be in excess of ablest sto up[?] Passes on expected. Sent from arrival of Bolter, had experts to purchase for Choc[?] Ship.	
27th	Saw DDGS 1st Army at Railhead & Advancing scheme of [?] munitions with [?] [?]. [?] of ammt after for rifle grenades. Saw Detach McCord Dur re learn of K.E.H. Dur.	
28th	Rubies received from 1st Army (that of w/o & Co B.T. arrived in accordance with Permanent rank). Troops re munitions supply maxim covering for R.E.D. stores at	
29th	Returning point. Saw OC K.G.S. & K.H. 11th Hat [?] depotage 2 Peus Persel[?]pac arrived for [?] Lancers. Arr Stores received from Base	

Army Form C. 2118.

WAR DIARY
or
INTELLIGENCE SUMMARY.
(Erase heading not required.)

Instructions regarding War Diaries and Intelligence Summaries are contained in F.S. Regs., Part II. and the Staff Manual respectively. Title pages will be prepared in manuscript.

Hour, Date, Place	Summary of Events and Information	Remarks and references to Appendices
BETHUNE. 30th April.	14 Travelling Kitchens arrived Railhead & issued to 2nd Bn. Highland. Ordered 15 pairs of trace cols of britt instead. Enough with regt training Office. Reported B16 Corps actually in Training supplies of leather for Boot Res, head Rpr. and worktops — also Bandages. 30.4.16	Endorsed Major R.V.O. DADOS 2don Divn

121/6023

47th Division

DADOS. 47th Division

Vol III

May & June 1915

WAR DIARY
INTELLIGENCE SUMMARY.
(Erase heading not required.)

Army Form C. 2118.

Confidential

War Diary of
D.A.D.O.S.
47th Division

From 1-5-15.
To 30-6-15.

WAR DIARY
or
INTELLIGENCE SUMMARY.
(Erase heading not required.)

Army Form C. 2118.

Hour, Date, Place.	Summary of Events and Information	Remarks and references to Appendices
BETHUNE 1st May.	5000 cot comforters received for distribution in lieu of pants for use against cold by future issue. Also 2500 to be sent by lorry received from Dep. Supply Column for 1st Div. south.	
2nd	2 photographers with telescopic depths received & distributed in accordance with instructions of D.S.	
	10 Travelling Kitchens received for 17th, 18th & 1st Batts. Visited Roux factory re grenade carriers.	
3rd.	10 T. Kitchens received for 19th, 20th & 21st Batts. Porridge ash annoying from Roux – plans over Roux factory	
n 100 –	Ordered to have order for head mustard	
	Went ESTAIRES re purchase of grenade carriers. Owing to non suitability waste – ordered 1500 and	
4th.	5000 more comforters from Base. Samples of grenade carriers received – satisfactory. 50 required for each Batt. 250 to Cyclists. Ordered whipcord on hand & cots complete. Also lorry at the use against asphyxiating gas. Visited Beauvaipre in enquiry.	

WAR DIARY
or
INTELLIGENCE SUMMARY.
(Erase heading not required.)

Army Form C. 2118.

Hour, Date, Place	Summary of Events and Information	Remarks and references to Appendices
BETHUNE 4th May.	Visits GORRE. re MKV waistcoats 19th La Bassée intk. t.o.m. K.V. Corps. Took fures body crashed. Two their Deliberately aby woods of Zuri.	
5th	Lt T Kitchen for 2nd Batt received gathers utilised from KNVRE left received moved HAVRE and BOULOGNE Motor 43. 2nd M Bde - re Grenade Rifles Springebos issued me French cart and tray carts to 6th & 9th Bdes. Received instructions to proceed 12.	
6th	July. T Kitchen issued fr 21b. 22nd & 23rd Battn. Body loads ets for asphyxiating gases. Orders issued by funds GOC/69 to attend rot reported on. Purchased 15v/job for 5500 yrs etpt sandbags + cotton waste. freed officially in M. conv'ing army of Thane -	
7th	T. Kitchen fr 22 Batt arrived. Two complete Division Purchased Bromine gauze + cotton wake for pads fr while Division. Cdr for redirect works at at. Fr 22 E. B. Vandage. Also proceed 1728 metres have of tape. Issued 6 more trench mortar ah. To French 2nd 6 th Bdes. 20 sprayers sent Thornophoth Sodas. card fm 16 Corps + dis	

Army Form C. 2118.

WAR DIARY
or
INTELLIGENCE SUMMARY.
(Erase heading not required.)

12

Instructions regarding War Diaries and Intelligence Summaries are contained in F.S. Regs., Part II. and the Staff Manual respectively. Title pages will be prepared in manuscript.

Place	Hour, Date.	Summary of Events and Information	Remarks and references to Appendices
BETHUNE	8 May.	Large convoy wound stores received. Issued to units where possible by units. Where opportunity offered. Pinched and cordoys for carrying spare etc. Braces, canvas delivered — distributed 1st & 4th Bns & 3 Batt. 5th Essex Bde. unable to get at 2/3rd Batt. 4th Royal Warwick carts for 4th (Hunts) Bde handed over by order of Morning & delivered & also balance (4 carts) of London Bde.	
	9th —	Heavy fighting — at times the army roads to com. Task. Advance of stores at Railhead + distribution as possible. especially Vouchers to RaRo available. a remainder of Bivouacs convoy to Motor car taken for personal use of Staff of Division.	
	10th —	Meat and wine removed allowed up for Depots. Sent out time with same for 2nd & 2/4th Battalion. Rawanpage troops v. late. Urgent priority for polos to route to avoid forks hand wheel sheaving for 4.5 in. How. 15 m wearing lasts "repair of Luton." Notified C.O. that Park Ministers/ divers be arranged tonight a/c army 2 rounds that there now tout	

13.

WAR DIARY
or
INTELLIGENCE SUMMARY.
(Erase heading not required.)

Army Form C. 2118.

Hour, Date, Place	Summary of Events and Information	Remarks and references to Appendices
BETHUNE. 10th May (cont)	Moved as much as possible. Suffering acute internal pains & was to A.D.S. Unable to obtain transport, ambulance returned to BETHUNE.	
11th "		
Bethune 12th May/15	Arrived from Abeele at 7.30pm from Major Ladbury. A.D.D. admitted to hospital with broken rib. Reported arrival, afterwards taking over office documents etc. Obtaining keys etc from Major Ludlow in hospital.	
13th "	Took a Richard, 2 o/c to Depot, examining into system of working each. Grave danger from Base via new route which shortens journey considerably. Bethune shelled at 11pm. 3 civilians killed in house opposite site of these being billets.	

WAR DIARY or INTELLIGENCE SUMMARY

Army Form C. 2118.

Hour, Date, Place	Summary of Events and Information	Remarks and references to Appendices
Bethune 14th Aug/15	Ordered 500 Bomb Carriers from Firm at Calais	
" 15th	Issued a./to.14. Since copies to 19th Battery. Purchased 12 Bowls of leather. 99 kilos at 9.25 a kilo for divisional shoemakers shop. 15 pr B.L.C. Gun in 20nd Battery condemned by I.O.M. demanded a replacement by telegram. A.D.O.S. Army Cattell Smith paid a visit but at time was visiting Major Audley in Hospital	
" 16th	Stores arrived artillery instead of clothing. Sent in error. P.T.O. in reply to my telegram and stores R'd arrived & had to send lorries at 6 p.m. to clear. G.O.C. R.A. reported that I.O.M. had condemned 36 Vents T. cond. for 15 pr B.L.C. Guns, being investigated. 36 foot ladder for G.O.C. R.A. for observation purposes made received today. Went to arrange for Batch arrival G.O.D.O.S. Army	

WAR DIARY
or
INTELLIGENCE SUMMARY

Army Form C. 2118.

Hour, Date, Place	Summary of Events and Information	Remarks and references to Appendices
Béthune 17th May 1915	Inspected Bookers of 19th Battalion. Exchanged 3 bolts from other carbines though Bore is inserviceable which had badly Gas & Bullets.	
" 18th "	Issued 119 Periscopes from Bomb Factory & issued same between 3 Brigades of Infantry. Fuzi Key badly wanted & Cuillos get them made and in line as at Bomb Factory. Wire Boot for Same. Also for Fuze. Picked 12 Bends of Leather for Shoemakers	
" 19th "	Saw I.O. & R. Vents who is carrying out an inspection of all 3 Brigades to ascertain exact position (promised help and confirmed) a 15pdr Gun condemned by I.O. in 19th Battery (Forster) demanded Estay.	
" 20th "	Railhead moved from Choques to Lillers 2 Wagons & 2 sets of search light arrived visioned to R.E. S.O.R.'s report on Vents reverses 19 inserviceable & 1 missing. Will take the large plug Gauge. Reported to O.D.O.S. A 15pdr Gun No 1150 of 19th Battery condemned & demanded	

16

WAR DIARY
or
INTELLIGENCE SUMMARY.

Army Form C. 2118.

(Erase heading not required.)

Hour, Date, Place	Summary of Events and Information	Remarks and references to Appendices
Bethune 21st Aug 1915	4 Tents & 20 Periscopes received. Tents wants badly. As G.O.M. has decided to obtain 300 Blankets 25 per Battalion for carrying wounded from trenches. Bethune being heavily shelled & dashing very near our office, one piece of shell coming through window.	
" 22nd "	Obtained 300 Blankets from No 4 Supply Train & all distributed to 12 Battalions before 10 am as ordered late last night. By means of 3 lorries. 1 Periscope reissued to Nos 12 B.C. for trial. Bethune again shelled & will move office tomorrow.	
" 23rd "	Moved into new office at Choques 2 ½ m of Bethune. Major Dudley not improving sent to hospital at Versailles. 6 "Martin" sights for short rifle received issued to No 1, 141 & 143rd Infantry Brigades, 2 each, for trial. Ordered to obtain 16 Short rifles per Battalion for purpose of firing rifle grenades, those with bulged barrels being suitable, to obtain from Rathent	

WAR DIARY or INTELLIGENCE SUMMARY

Army Form C. 2118.

Hour, Date, Place	Summary of Events and Information	Remarks and references to Appendices
Bethune 24 May 1915	Gale back mustin purchased for hyly Respirator. Firm Agreed to Give refund at price paid for its.	
25th	Interviewed Shoemakers for a purchase of muslin not to add for Respirator, new pattern to be issued in lieu of those made locally.	
26th	1st Battalion complained of rifles jamming, procured rifles & tested them, one was found to have an enlarged chamber due to constant cleaning, a rifle would, the cared expansion in case of an inch from base materially jamming. Exchanged rifle.	
27th	Rec'd 5 Bundles of muslin to Issue to Batln Meyer which could not be used for making Respirator as a hw pattern was introduced, obtained same & made pad for Reg't Fanes 317-55.	
28th	First supply of Smoke Helmets & Respirators received & distributed & demanded on Base full requirements of each catalog waiting for indent. 1 Rifle with telescope sight, & 6 "Ibantine" Sights arrived for trial Issued to Brigade, 2 each.	

17

18

Army Form C. 2118.

WAR DIARY
or
INTELLIGENCE SUMMARY.
(Erase heading not required.)

Hour, Date, Place	Summary of Events and Information	Remarks and references to Appendices
29th May 1915 Bethune	Excluded from Rations 50 rifle bay't Battalion to replace others bomb out G.O.C. Appointed a D.A.D.S. to Division vice Major Gen Bell D.S.O. The following letter of 27.5.1915: Attachments to the D.A.D.S. Transport cancelled. Base Inspects all Men to bring Cancelled	
30th "	Prior to 14th April Ware store still required on these Indent to be redemanded by units. Wrote C.O.O. Base agreeing to this	
31st "	Major Dudley evacuated from hospital & Sent to Base hospital at Boulogne Attended funeral of Brigadier General Hughes 141st Brigade. Killed in trenches 2 days previously. 1 Rifle with Telescope sight received issued to 142nd Brigade Suggestion of C.O. Base to cancel all indents from 6th April cancelled	

31st May 1915

F.A. Buckland Capt
D.A.D.O.S.
47th Division

Army Form C. 2118.

WAR DIARY
or
INTELLIGENCE SUMMARY.
(Erase heading not required.)

Instructions regarding War Diaries and Intelligence Summaries are contained in F. S. Regs., Part II. and the Staff Manual respectively. Title pages will be prepared in manuscript.

Place	Hour, Date.	Summary of Events and Information	Remarks and references to Appendices
Bethune	1st June 1915	Purchased 250 Boots (arrived at Estaires) Bethune still being shelled daily. Received Order to move had Quarters going to Terquin & refilling at the Regiment	
do	2nd June 15	Moved Office & Depot at 2.30 pm as ordered Gala day	
Terquin	3rd June 15	Depot a refilling point ready before office. the Canal be avoided, refilling was to from 7am. to bring Depot to Terquin a house to house would necessitate refilling at 10.30 pm.	
do	4th June 15	A 15/pr Gun Ns 1190 of 1/3 London Battery Conducued by S.O.S. & handed do.	
do	5th do	Saw S.O.S. at Terquin with Colnel Scott filter air 0 on waiting S.O.S re repair of	
do	6th do	6 Hyposcopic received issued 5 to V1 Section for trial.	

Army Form C. 2118.

WAR DIARY
or
INTELLIGENCE SUMMARY.
(Erase heading not required.)

Hour, Date, Place	Summary of Events and Information	Remarks and references to Appendices
Lerguin 7th June 1915	Sale of pieces of smoke helmets found to def? of Branch easily in rare packets, quite unsuitable. Soldiers initial name of 1000 having been typed. It got then consented by Contract for attached type to be supplied for the purpose.	
do 8th do	To Estaires for Bomb Carriers. Obtained enough that grenade Bombs and explained them to 2nd Quarter Gen. 51st Division	
do 9th do	Purchased French Carts to place other destroyed by shell fire. Two type guns sent to Base for 11901 & 11371 of 13th & 20th Batteries unserviceable	
do 10th do	3 Rifles with Optical Lights received issued to 140th, 141st & 142nd Brigades	

Army Form C. 2118.

WAR DIARY
or
INTELLIGENCE SUMMARY.
(Erase heading not required.)

Instructions regarding War Diaries and Intelligence
Summaries are contained in F.S. Regs., Part II.
and the Staff Manual respectively. Title pages
will be prepared in manuscript.

Hour, Date, Place	Summary of Events and Information	Remarks and references to Appendices
Verquin 11th June 1915	To Retaines for Bombarniers. Suddenly ordered to move to Soeur-le-Noue	
Noeux-les- 12th do Mines	do returned at same point. Telescope Refracteurs issued to 140th Bde for trial	
Soeux-le-Noue 13th do	11.00 O. Reporters arrived at St Omer from Boulogne. Sent 2 lorries to bring them to Depot.	
do 14th do	To Etaine for water trough	
do 15th do	Shell dropped on office roof, &c &c & has been fired at a Tank. Penetrates through first floor nearly through second floor, one Civilian injured slightly. This occurred at 4.30am G.S. Fitzpatrick	
do 16th do	Instructions transferred to a new Establishment to come out again with a new Brigade	

WAR DIARY
or
INTELLIGENCE SUMMARY.

Army Form C. 2118.

Nouex les Mines 18th June 1915

Hour, Date, Place	Summary of Events and Information	Remarks and references to Appendices
	Major _____ appeared in London Gazette as 2nd Lieutenant (Temporary) dated from 21st June 1915	
do 18th do	To Neuville re transfer of a Trench Disinfector to London Church Station Hostataire bar also trough & Bomb Carrier	
do 19th do	Failed to obtain any suitable boot for cans to Batterie as a book cart, all doing too purchased by French Brigadoshmaid got allegate & The	
do 20 do	Went to learn parts to 15th Battery re purchase of a book cart. To many to fill draughts due to 5th Column, no good to be purchased in Bethune & myself ineffective rifle accoutrement to 141st Brigade for trial	
do 21st do	To Souville & purchased 12 pieces of oak for many Polo draughts, also Rifle Covers. Went to Chocquer to hire a stove for storage of Reserve & Reparation squads to Relaide Arranged for withdrawal of Blankets from Division Commencing at 10 am	

WAR DIARY
or
INTELLIGENCE SUMMARY.
(Erase heading not required.)

Army Form C. 2118.

Instructions regarding War Diaries and Intelligence Summaries are contained in F.S. Regs., Part II. and the Staff Manual respectively. Title pages will be prepared in manuscript.

Hour, Date, Place	Summary of Events and Information	Remarks and references to Appendices
Nœux-les-Mines 22/6/1915	Took in Blankets. Sent 20 Catapults, 10 ex 25 + 10 to "B" Section. On trial	
do 23rd do	Took in balance of Blankets. When returned they are to be sent to G.O. Paris, not more than one truck per day after making previous arrangements with the D.A.D.T.	
do 24th do	First Truck of Blankets sent to Paris today. To Mazingarbe for Rifle Covers & Specimens Water Bucket, Canvas for trench use	
do 25th do	Third Truck of Blankets sent to Paris. Discussed Rocket at H.Q. De re Bucket to Carry Canvas for carrying drinking water up to trenches & decided to purchase 200 for trial. 1 Telescopic rifle received. Issued to 2nd Bn The Ind Batt. To Mazeuille to test 200 Buckets on trial	
do 26th do	Orders received to withdraw rifle bayonets from all Canadians except the Divnl Supply Column at once. To Ex'l numbers to Base. All other rifles & supply columns to be issued & armed with Carbines. (Cavalry Supply Columns armed with Carbines but not with Carbine ammn)	

Army Form C. 2118.

WAR DIARY
or
INTELLIGENCE SUMMARY.
(Erase heading not required.)

Instructions regarding War Diaries and Intelligence Summaries are contained in F.S. Regs., Part II. and the Staff Manual respectively. Title pages will be prepared in manuscript.

Hour, Date, Place			Summary of Events and Information	Remarks and references to Appendices
Soucis le Mons	24/9/15		Bivo. Day. Depot that is laid up with acct of врд. Defourd Railhead would be moved tomorrow	
do	25th	do	Railhead changed from Choques to Lillers today. Handed in the balance of blankets for same at Choques instead of Lillers agreed to by R.T.O.	
do	29th	do	Withdrew 56 Rifles & bayonets from Supply Column & sent them to Base from Driver. Conversed with O(a)C regarding withdrawal & transfer of blankets wagons &c. Purchased 200 bottles of foresty. Pigeons one bomb line for 142 Brigade. Took over hired stone at Choques & placed in it 10,000 Reprisals 30 schedule Inade.	

25

Army Form C. 2118.

WAR DIARY
or
INTELLIGENCE SUMMARY.
(Erase heading not required.)

Instructions regarding War Diaries and Intelligence
Summaries are contained in F.S. Regs., Part II.
and the Staff Manual respectively. Title pages
will be prepared in manuscript.

Hour, Date, Place	Summary of Events and Information	Remarks and references to Appendices
Noeux-les-Mines 30 June 1915	Reports unfavourably regarding a suggestion for the appointment of a Boot Inspector at the Front. Took over a new of the Brigade Commander to there move a quid-stand by against 40 Yds issued Brigade of Infantry Rs etc for trial with Observers	

Noeux-les-Mines
30 June 1915

F.H. Buckland Major
D.A.D.O.S
1st Div

DOS

18/6/49

47th Division

DADOS. 47th Division

Vol IV

Army Form C. 2118.

WAR DIARY
~~INTELLIGENCE SUMMARY.~~
(Erase heading not required.)

Instructions regarding War Diaries and Intelligence Summaries are contained in F.S. Regs., Part II. and the Staff Manual respectively. Title pages will be prepared in manuscript.

Hour, Date, Place	Summary of Events and Information	Remarks and references to Appendices
	Confidential. War Diary of:- D.A.D. of 47th Division. (Major F.N. Buckland) a.o.d. From :- 1-7-15. To :- 31-7-15.	

26

Army Form C. 2118.

WAR DIARY
or
INTELLIGENCE SUMMARY.
(Erase heading not required.)

Instructions regarding War Diaries and Intelligence Summaries are contained in F.S. Regs., Part II. and the Staff Manual respectively. Title pages will be prepared in manuscript.

Hour, Date, Place	Summary of Events and Information	Remarks and references to Appendices
Noeux-les-Mines 1st July 1915	To Estaires for Bout Barrow & Berwick for Buckets water for company drinking water to the trenches. Rated capacity Bedford 35 8 Karriers lent Quantis allowed to come too to be 11685 lbs. Sent sections for trial repair.	
2nd July 1915	Took up 200 Buckets water to Head Qrs of 141st Inf Brigade for trial reported to about 141st Brigade Headquarters & the 142nd Brigade at Bethune. Disbursed section of 5 cable telephones with Major Alexander, detachment of S.O.S. started to lay West Lateral Paveau at 9.30 am onwards.	
3rd July 1915	To Rutland. Met General Paraoin & Colonel Weir Smith at Villers discussed various points re best method of dealing with Ammo store on arrival at Rutland from the Front. Cars proceeded to disposal of. An additional N.C.O. officer was required for duty at Rutland.	

Army Form C. 2118.

WAR DIARY
or
INTELLIGENCE SUMMARY.
(Erase heading not required.)

Hour, Date, Place	Summary of Events and Information	Remarks and references to Appendices
Nieuwe-les-Dunes 4 July 1915	Took a Bde fatigue to Head Quarters and explained the working of it. German helmet has captured by the 5th Battalion (London) arrived back from base after conversion. Issued to Regiment. 4 pairs of "Gloepacks" boots arrived for trial with men who are constantly working in mud & slush. These were issued to R.E. men whose heel shoes wetted 6 day	
5th July 1915	Interviewed Lt Col Ra at Maringasten re award for a hat for Trench mortar Battery. This matter is not self contained & its equipment is manufactured under consideration; for the present it cannot obtain stores from this to which it is attached except for technical stores which is supplied by D.A.D.O.S. Also interviewed at Saint Pierre Col [illegible] Brigade dumped for 16 Barrels for storing water in the keep in trenches for drinking purposes. Discussed the same question later at	

Army Form C. 2118.

WAR DIARY
or
INTELLIGENCE SUMMARY.
(Erase heading not required.)

Instructions regarding War Diaries and Intelligence Summaries are contained in F.S. Regs., Part II. and the Staff Manual respectively. Title pages will be prepared in manuscript.

Hour, Date, Place	Summary of Events and Information	Remarks and references to Appendices

Neuve Chapelle
5th July 1915

as these Quarters of Division when it was decided to use fetal twine, being cheaper, more easy to obtain more readily. Saddle sheepskins.

The question of Respirators for horses approved for of by 1st Army. These bags, Boyes's cotton waste & Soap & Solution to be carried in a tin, the whole carried round horses neck.

Units all ordered to ascertain the number of horses they have & all should be equipped with a respirator.

Smith Miller accidentally trampled on by a horse fractured both tem. 16th takes

6th July 1915

Went to 6 Cd D.O. of 140th Bde at Bonnegarde 1st1st Bde at Le Drelio & with No 243 removed Sprayers on issue on loan to 1st Division, all 5 Sprayers on issue on loan to 2d Bde for an overhaul were to parade took them to Bde for an overhaul

7th July 1915

Went to Bouvigne & Le Drebis and inspected all Vermorel Sprayers in the 10 & 2d Sections all in good condition except 1 which was taken to Shop for overhaul. Also taking knozzles chiefly at fault.

(73989) W4141-463. 400,000. 9/14. H.&J. Ltd. Forms/C. 2118/10.

WAR DIARY
or
INTELLIGENCE SUMMARY.
(Erase heading not required.)

Army Form C. 2118.

Hour, Date, Place	Summary of Events and Information	Remarks and references to Appendices
Jouy-le-Monts 7th July/15	The rubber washers are rent badly like Nothing appears to suffer so badly through contact with depôt solution. Demanded Parts, amm[unitio]n. to meet probable demands. Reports from Brigade re number of reparations considered necessary for horses. G.O.C. Division & decided up R.A. Brigade: Batteries each.	
8th July/15	Activities got back too to carry solution for horse respirators	
9th July/15	Went to Aire for acetate sufficient to make 1000 kg of pieces for our 4 Reliefs.	
10th July/15	Inspected broken G/7th Battalion (found) 3 had the axles broken, one badly, & dent all in to Shops. One is a very weak part of the Cart, as also are the wheels.	

Army Form C. 2118.

WAR DIARY
or
INTELLIGENCE SUMMARY.
(Erase heading not required.)

Instructions regarding War Diaries and Intelligence
Summaries are contained in F. S. Regs., Part II.
and the Staff Manual respectively. Title pages
will be prepared in manuscript.

Hour, Date, Place	Summary of Events and Information	Remarks and references to Appendices

Locre les Tombe

11th July 1915

No 2 Duplicates of Machine Gun being available at Base Carpets. Gun arrived in lieu for 1st London Battalion. Issued in the afternoon. 3 Rifles with telescope sights arrived & issued to 140, 141 & 142nd Inf Bde to be tried out with Sharpshooters.

Town shelled today.

12th July 15

Report re .303 2a. Cases of V-15 manufacture, these were actually operated on rough cut with a knife about ¼ of an inch from base then

[diagram of cartridge]

fired to round rapidly, result quite satisfactory. Obtained some Ammunition Rifled. Report sent to Head Quarters 4th Corps with damaged carted 9th Case 205 in damaged case.

Colonel Battens with 2nd Bde to arrived at Head Quarters of Division to discuss question of 2 lb. armour Cartridge Cases. He accompanied him to H.Q. of 141st Inf Bde at St. Jeohants Vaccangaebs on formation of discussion at Div. M. Quitter

(73989) W4141—463. 400,000. 9/14. H.&J.Ltd. Forms/C. 2118/10.

Army Form C. 2118.

WAR DIARY
or
INTELLIGENCE SUMMARY.
(Erase heading not required.)

Instructions regarding War Diaries and Intelligence Summaries are contained in F.S. Regs., Part II. and the Staff Manual respectively. Title pages will be prepared in manuscript.

31

Hour, Date, Place	Summary of Events and Information	Remarks and references to Appendices
Source-les-Mines 12.7.1915	Ordered to move out of Sourse-les-Mines to Marles-les-Mines but 12 noon tomorrow. This order was cancelled at 12 M n	
do 13 July 1915	A railhead 2nd Division damaged wagon lumber belonging to 2nd Battalion (Co. of London) as result of an accident. Wired O/C to demand parts to replace. Received orders same day.	
do 14 July 1915	To Greenay, to 2nd Lt O/C 18 2nd Battery re purchase of a book. Batt. O/C agreed to hold one rather than purchase a new pattern as Battery one selected	
do 15 July 1915	Sergt Hugo A O/C reported arrival for purpose of instruction as brigade bombing officer for about 3 weeks	

(73989) W4141–463. 400,000. 9/14. H.&J.Ltd. Forms/C. 2118/10.

WAR DIARY
or
INTELLIGENCE SUMMARY.
(Erase heading not required.)

Army Form C. 2118.

Instructions regarding War Diaries and Intelligence Summaries are contained in F.S. Regs., Part II. and the Staff Manual respectively. Title pages will be prepared in manuscript.

Hour, Date, Place	Summary of Events and Information	Remarks and references to Appendices
Nouvelle Eglise 16.7.15	Merville to order Bomb barrows & 6 wire coils to order Rifle covers. 10th Brigade complained their Bombs were no good, not of the 95 mm trench mortar. Obtained the Mortar Manual on being that the Home bomb fitted correctly, reported & we added some local fillers, bombs must be no percussion but those issued from Ammunition train.	
do 19th July 1915	32 Vermorel Sprayers arrived viewed to "O" N.Z. Section. & No less than 12 of these Sprayers had the Taps broken off in transit. Reported the faulty method of packing to 6.0.0. Base. Had all taps based and refitted in G.O.D. Shop. G.0.0 Base direct 6.0 S. Base to procure? Suitable for importation for repair, located at no 3 1st Army for instructions or of some other suitable substitute should be locally obtained.	

Army Form C. 2118.

WAR DIARY
or
INTELLIGENCE SUMMARY.
(Erase heading not required.)

32

Instructions regarding War Diaries and Intelligence Summaries are contained in F. S. Regs., Part II. and the Staff Manual respectively. Title pages will be prepared in manuscript.

Place	Date	Hour	Summary of Events and Information	Remarks and references to Appendices
Noeux les Mines	16th July 1915		Failed changed to Fusiliers from riflers from this morning. D.A.R. Order issued for 4.5" Howitzer, Hollo Grenade & Pitcher Grenade empty boxes to be returned to Ammunition Railhead. Saw shells today.	
do	17"		To Estaires & Doulieu to get Bomb Carriers & Rifle Covers. Issued 300 Bucket units canvas for French use.	
do	22"		Shoemakers rather less in stock & repairable boots diminished. Order issued directing units to return boots for repair regularly. If large numbers are sent in at one lot every few days the rush, it is impossible to work the Shoemakers shop to the best advantage. Returning a red cloth Grenade badge for distinguishing Bomb throwers as too samples one de one mounted on black cloth (one other on khaki, the latter preferred. Badge about 3"× 1¾" to be worn LA. instructions from 1st Army received directing withdrawal of rifles from all Battery & Brigade hqrs to pr Battery forwards. Also to exchange those with Brigade Ammunition Column to Divisional Ammunition Columns. Proposed transfers as personnel, 1 Field Ambulance, a S.6 personnel, for rifles as sights for Th. LA. all concerned. Ammunition begins of R & R.S. to be withdrawn. Saddles for officers for Gun & Technical	

1577 Wt.W10791/1773 500,000 1/15 D.D.& L. A.P.S.S./Forms/C. 2118.

Army Form C. 2118.

34.

Instructions regarding War Diaries and Intelligence Summaries are contained in F. S. Regs., Part II. and the Staff Manual respectively. Title pages will be prepared in manuscript.

WAR DIARY
or
INTELLIGENCE SUMMARY.
(Erase heading not required.)

Place	Date	Hour	Summary of Events and Information	Remarks and references to Appendices
Noeux-les-Mines	21st July 1915		D.D.o.S. 1st Army wrote to G.H.Q. as the number of 15 pr B.L.C. Guns in Division that are nearing state of condemnation with a view to bring replaced by others from 48th Division who are being rearmed with 15pr BLguns. Handed over direct to 140th, 141st, 142nd Brigade, 3. of 2 Battle Sights for use with Machine Guns; also 2 Vernier Sprayers 6 sets to sections. Telegraphed to D.D.o.S. 1st Army that Gun Nos 1127; 1073; 1150; 1190 & 1147 had been returned to the Base unserviceable. That 15pr Guns Nos 1121; 1207; 1148 & 1081 were nearing condemnation & would also require replacing of Battle Sights for Machine Guns. first issue, armed & issued proportionately to the 3 Infantry Brigades. 16 Shields to 35th outstanding to 5 Sharpshooter Brigade & as 1st Army called for full report, rendered at once all that was obtainable from Sections. 3 Vickers Guns arrived & issued 2 to 6th & 1 to 6/8th Battalion. Complete 64 Gun basis. Discussed question at Abed Quarters concerning question of Respirators for horses being Cancelled.	
do	22nd	do		

WAR DIARY
or
INTELLIGENCE SUMMARY.

Army Form C. 2118.

Place	Date	Hour	Summary of Events and Information	Remarks and references to Appendices
Noeux-les-Mines	23rd July/15		To Bacingarbe & Vce-Brebis to No 4 & 141st Brigade with 5 disposeupo Epilattier Sinocope pattern for trial Early report. To Annville obtained 300 Buckets to be Carried forward for carrying water up to the trenches, issued after nightfall	
do	24th	do	4 Battalions brought up to 4 Machine Guns each Coris by receipt of 4 Vickers Guns today for Nos 168, 1170, 1172, 1182, 1261, 1179, 1182, 1261, 1179, 541, 1176 Vickers to 1/15th, 1/16th, 1/17th & 1/18th Battalions 2 each respectively. 1 Light Tripod & 1 Scaffolding Shading Shanks allowed Each Infantry Battalion extra to other Equipment. demand submitted	
do	25th	do	Went to Bacingarbe & Vce-Brebis to discuss most suitable barrels to place in the 4 Keeps of "C" & "D" sections of trenches, then to No. 2nd Bn. a large cask considered most suitable to hold about 56 gallons of drinking water.	

36.

Army Form C. 2118.

WAR DIARY
or
INTELLIGENCE SUMMARY.
(Erase heading not required.)

Place	Date	Hour	Summary of Events and Information	Remarks and references to Appendices
Noeux-les-Mines	26th July 15		Arranged for purchase of 16 Casks of 56 gallons each. Shop to have 2 Casks on roughly 2 gallons of oats for horses in each shop.	
do	27th		6 loads of 28 timbers with lorries arrived. Issued to 7th & 17th Battalions to complete Machine Guns to 4 per Battalion. Consignment of smoke shields arrived which completed the Reserve of 1 per Officer & man.	
do	28th		A Salvage Company has been formed in the Division with three sub depots posted in different localities for the purpose of recovering all stores left in trenches, billets etc etc. The men at the Sub Depots collect & retain as a Depot from whence the recovered arms, accoutrements etc will be despatched to the Base. The Cook of this Company is bound to produce excellent results. 16 Casks 56 gallons, purchased. Issued for use in Shops.	

WAR DIARY
or
INTELLIGENCE SUMMARY.

Army Form C. 2118.

Place	Date	Hour	Summary of Events and Information	Remarks and references to Appendices
Noeux-les-Mines	28 July 1915		Continued. Red cloth badge for Bomb & Grenade throwers badge to take the form of a Grenade. 600 demanded, purchased outside cloth roughly and a design of Grenades are being made in Divisional Tailors shop.	
do.	29th	"	Discussed question of Baths for men on coming out of trenches, for men refitting. Also best means of cleaning clothing & destroying vermin. Barrels cut in half to make tubs were sugdt & rations for killing vermin. Orders given or received to arrange for purchase.	
do	30th	"	Orders received regarding the withdrawal of Rifles & Bayonet from Sердs in Div of a Quarter Officers Servants & Grooms in Divisl Hd Qrs of 2 Dy Rs, Div Signal Company; Sanitary Section; Mobile Veterinary Section, Kalarys Company, No Officer Mules with Field Post Offices. Divisional Routine Order issued regarding withdrawal.	

Army Form C. 2118.

WAR DIARY
or
INTELLIGENCE SUMMARY.
(Erase heading not required.)

Place	Date	Hour	Summary of Events and Information	Remarks and references to Appendices
Noeux les Mines	29 July 15		Went to Braudgarde & purchased 53 barrels from a Brewery. R.S. Company who went on the spas, got O.C.'s permission for his men to have them in. Left pray to Beaing at 8.30 pm. Tubs for bathing purpose. Purchased 163 flys wire now after much difficulty, these are required for killing vermin in mens clothes. Have to be used during the time they are having a bath.	

Noeux-les-Mines
1st August 1915

F.A. Muellandajor S.
D.A.D.D.S.
27th Div.

47th K warin

121/6754

DADOS. 47th Division
Vol V
August. 15

Army Form C. 2118.

WAR DIARY
INTELLIGENCE SUMMARY.
(Erase heading not required.)

Instructions regarding War Diaries and Intelligence Summaries are contained in F. S. Regs., Part II. and the Staff Manual respectively. Title pages will be prepared in manuscript.

Hour, Date, Place	Summary of Events and Information	Remarks and References to Appendices
	Confidential War Diary of D.A.D.O.S. 47th Division. (Major Buckland. A.O.D) From :- 1. 8. 15 To :- 31. 8. 15	

[Stamp: BASE A.O.D. 6 SEP. 1915]

WAR DIARY or **INTELLIGENCE SUMMARY**

Army Form C. 2118
D.a.D.O.S. of Division (London)

Place	Date	Hour	Summary of Events and Information	Remarks and references to Appendices
Souverlie Mines	1st Aug 1916		Received 4 Battle Lights for Bacon Guns from D.a.D.O.S. 15th Division. Issued to Battalions. Went to Snaregarbe to see S. of Bony Rs. 2nd canvas funnel, in hall which were ordered on 3rd July, found they had arranged two lorries to refilling point. Blenery badly shelled whilst there. Recent Enquiries to attach the Respirators stored at Bacorne ordered. Reserves held over to Corps to remove to Division area. 1st Corps approved of him storing a at Blacquo. During the period the Divisional Laundries shop has been opened Buy 5th April to 31.7.16 by the undermentioned shows what has been done:- The personnel consists of 29 December withdrawn from various Units of the Division viz R.a. 2, R.E. 1, Infantry 26 Total 6. 2 = 29. Re Laundries are distributed for work as follows:- 1 Sergt. I/Charg.; 1 Starching; 1 Buttons; 1 Ironing & 1 Evening; 2 at the bench Labeling etc 1 + 1 Cook = 29.	36

WAR DIARY
or
INTELLIGENCE SUMMARY.
(Erase heading not required.)

Army Form C. 2118

Place	Date	Hour	Summary of Events and Information	Remarks and references to Appendices
Havre	1st Aug/15		The repairs carried out during the shop has been opened are as under:—	

Boots Soled Heeled etc.   Boots Condemned   Remarks

Month	Boots Soled Heeled etc	Boots Condemned	Remarks
5th to 30th April/15	1158	85	Other repairs,
" 31st May "	1961	210	such as Harness,
" 30th June "	2841	527	Saddlery, and
" 31st July "	2132	584	Equipment have
Totals	8092	1906	been done occasionally

A Tailors shop was also opened about the same time as the Shoemakers shop. The personnel consisting of 1 Corporal & 15 men. The work carried is as under:—

Suits of Clothing Repaired = Greatcoats = Jackets = Trousers Ld. Putters &c

April 1/15			25	104	125	10
May "			22	204	152	7
June "				258	278	50
July "				260	230	29
Total			47	826	635	98

Army Form C. 2118

WAR DIARY
or
INTELLIGENCE SUMMARY.

(Erase heading not required.)

Place	Date	Hour	Summary of Events and Information	Remarks and references to Appendices

Noeux-les-Mines	1 Aug 1915		The Tailors also assisted in the first opening of the Divisional Laundry repaired a large number of Kilts etc. Some Paribald Bags for Grenadier Companies were also made in the month of July.
			
			 Divisional Laundry
			 The wash carried out in the Divisional Laundry during the month of July was as follows:-
			
			          Received Sent
			 Shirts 32.000 29.000
			 Drawers 11.000 10.000
			 Vests 3.000 680
			 Socks 18.000 21.000
			      Total 64.000 60.680
			
			 Dirty Wagons are often sent by Units to draw clean mills clothing from the Laundry, these wagons are at times in a revenue condition.	

Army Form C. 2118

WAR DIARY
or
INTELLIGENCE SUMMARY.
(Erase heading not required.)

Place	Date	Hour	Summary of Events and Information	Remarks and references to Appendices
Leeway	1st Aug/15		Units have complained that clean underclothing issued from laundry are at times not entirely free from lice. It can only be assumed that clothing so affected is through the use of vermimous cars or vehicles which is used to draw the clean clothing. To obviate this the vehicles detailed a vermimous state are cleaned, washed & disinfected. To overcome the lice pest every article of clothing is subjected to a temperature of between 235°–240° for 30 minutes at least. They are washed & brushed & if necessary & before being placed into laundry stock are re-examined. After passing through this process the detection of a dead particle or a dead [insect] should not be sufficient to condemn the article. Experiments with blank containing ferticuli ova after being through the "Thresh" machine, have been worn for several days without causing any ill effects or producing any evidence that the ova are not dead.	

Army Form C. 2118

WAR DIARY
or
INTELLIGENCE SUMMARY.
(Erase heading not required.)

Place	Date	Hour	Summary of Events and Information	Remarks and references to Appendices
Nouveau-les-Mines	2nd Aug/15		Same length of hose as 6 after 3 weeks instruction pending appointment to a Brigade as subconductors left for home via above. Selected a store for depot at Gosnay prior to Division coming out of action to rest refit on the 4 instant.	S.A.
do	3rd	do	Nothing of importance to record	
Gosnay	4th	do	Lt. Col. Newnes-Brines at 8am for Gosnay on account of Division coming out of action for rest refitting. Horse depot to be designed at Gosnay bridge my own office to be as a refilling point all to be one building found the Rector of Gunchstraete Helpmaten stored at	S.A.

Army Form C. 2118

WAR DIARY
or
INTELLIGENCE SUMMARY.
(Erase heading not required.)

Place	Date	Hour	Summary of Events and Information	Remarks and references to Appendices
Continued				
Doimy	4 Aug/15		Baraques were completely transferred to-day. 104 Suits for men to the 11b2 Bn. one for killing lice. New clothing was distributed this afternoon by Depot Envie 6. Vickers machine guns arrived to-day for the 19th and 104 Battalions. 2 each. Reg. No's 1253 4659; 1677 1621; 1633/1260.	End
Doimy	5th	do	Issued 6 each of the 3 Infantry Brigade to 151 Bn 2nd. for Grenadier Companies. Vickers machine guns arrived. Issued 2 each to the 22nd & 23rd Battalions Reg. No's 1245 & 1262 & 1261 & 1269. to 15th Bd. 6 guns arrived to & placed as Confirmed Sent to the East viewed as follows:- To the 13th Battery Reg. No's 1789, 1329; 19th Battery Reg. No 1303 & the 20th Battery Reg. No 1077. To Howville for 500 Rifle Course about 3 days previously. Corporal Adams evacuated from hospital to the Base & afterwards for his release also that of Pte Miller who was unable to be sent back on 6/7/15	End

Army Form C. 2118

WAR DIARY
or
INTELLIGENCE SUMMARY
(Erase heading not required.)

Place	Date	Hour	Summary of Events and Information	Remarks and references to Appendices
Gonay	6 Aug/15		A good deal of leave/clothing &c. arrived during last 3 days. The Brigade quartered some distance away sent ours out to meet train to arrive to relieve congested state of depots. No vehicles recommended for appointment of acting Corporal to Indian Corps.	Feb
do	7th	do	The condition of latrine houses extremely great. The supply of water is limited, washing is done chiefly hats of buckets. Proceeded to Doenville Petaine to arrange purchase of some canvas troughs. Purchased 3 small microscopes for examining men from pediculus vera before safer treatment in the laundry. Clothing &c. Enoko helmets, a specially treated pattern is shortly to be issued, but for the present canonly 6 allowed for each Gun detachment consists of only 6 to a decided to demand 30 per Battalion. 360 demanded.	Feb

WAR DIARY
INTELLIGENCE SUMMARY
(Erase heading not required.)

Army Form C. 2118

Place	Date	Hour	Summary of Events and Information	Remarks and references to Appendices
Gosnay	8-Aug/15		Further instructions received regarding the issue of a Second Smoke Helmet to all formations at the Front	Ets
do	do		13,500 Smoke Helmets received from Base & issued to complete the 3rd Smoke Helmet for Officers & men	
		15.150 Smoke Helmets (the Pattern demanded to complete Division with 3 per Officer & man viz 2 to be carried & the third held in Reserve) by A.D.O.		
		Be much difficulty carrying on the person being one in a pocket, sewn on to the left flank of the jacket, the second one in a Satchel.		
		Satchels have not yet arrived & no action will be taken to issue the second Helmets until they are received. Respirators will be used as soon as a 2nd Officers issue is in possession of a second helmet.		
		12 G.S. Limbered Wagons arrived to-day which complete 11 Battalions out of 12 with 4 Limber Limbers for Machine Guns	Ets

Army Form C. 2118

WAR DIARY
or
INTELLIGENCE SUMMARY
(Erase heading not required.)

Place	Date	Hour	Summary of Events and Information	Remarks and references to Appendices
Doornay	9th Aug/15		Chance for tethering horses may be raised as tenants of sheds(?) for those horses which who had destroyed the ropes etc. A divisional order issued to that effect.	SA
do	10th	do	2 hotchkiss(?) arrived for 20th & 22nd Battery, the complete all Head Qrs V Battery of Brigade in the Division. A similar car for 15th Battalion also arrived. Eye fringe(?) for Division arrived & distributed 2 Vickers machine guns demanded with wheels, harness etc. for the 21st Battalion, this will complete all Battalions with 4 guns.	
do	11th	do	To decide Vetaine(?) to purchase trough & pickets for purpose of watering horses which is a serious question as causes considerable congestion of the road under present conditions. Trough & pickets will be completed on the 13th August.	SA

Army Form C. 2118

WAR DIARY
or
INTELLIGENCE SUMMARY

(Erase heading not required.)

Instructions regarding War Diaries and Intelligence Summaries are contained in F. S. Regs., Part II. and the Staff Manual respectively. Title Pages will be prepared in manuscript.

Place	Date	Hour	Summary of Events and Information	Remarks and references to Appendices
Lebucy	12th Aug/15		First consignment of 1,005 Suede helmets (tube pattern) arrived today for issue to the Machine gun detachments, also 500 of the new pattern satchel for carrying same.	
do	13th	do	Above cancelled. Orders received to issue to the 1st Division. Helmets withdrawn & issued to 1st Division. Orders then withdrawn from 1st Division & partly issued to units again	
do	14th	do	Orders now received from O.O. 1st Corps that every Suede helmet & the pattern satchel not be issued until the Expeditionary instructions. Helmets again withdrawn.	
do	15th	do	Two limbered wagons arrived for 24th Battalion. Was fully equipped by Division with uniforms for battalion. 1000 satchels for Suede helmets received. Issued dirty underclothing for exchange. Has been sent to laundry after dark, this is inconvenient. Divisional Routine Order received to present same after 6.30 p.m.	

WAR DIARY
or
INTELLIGENCE SUMMARY.

(Erase heading not required.)

Army Form C. 2118

Place	Date	Hour	Summary of Events and Information	Remarks and references to Appendices
Sotrenz	16th Aug/15		400 Flannel Helmets received. Issued to all O.R. for use with 10% of above, against gas attack, reserves to firing line. First issue	
do	17th	do	Acting 2nd Corporal Hinkham left for duty with the O.C. 3rd Corps Troops H.Q. against the rank of acting Sergeant. Private Sheldon arrived for duty in relief of Acting 2nd Corporal Hinkham	
do	18th	do	125 Smoke Helmets arrived, late pattern, the complete reissue for the Machine Gun detachments ordered to be equipped first.	
do	19th	do	} Nothing of importance to record.	
do	20th	do	}	
do	21st	do	}	
do	22nd	do	Gas expert lectured on the new Smoke Helmets, late pattern, Lews to apply, advantage etc. Also 500 copies of instructions for distribution. PB	

Army Form C. 2118

WAR DIARY
or
INTELLIGENCE SUMMARY.
(Erase heading not required.)

Place	Date	Hour	Summary of Events and Information	Remarks and references to Appendices
Bosany	23rd Aug/15		Satchels issued for carrying Lurche Helmets. Pattern not to be altered. Regimentally to have a flap now button hole inserted in the sling so as to prevent the bag dragging downwards of the spare end. No use the strain on the button. 28th Divisional Routine Orders inserted.	
do	24th	do		
do	25th	do	Today of importance to record	
do	26th	do	832 Satchels for Smoke Helmets, take pattern, arrived & obey Vicomt. 360 Smoke Helmets, take pattern, issued to lay for use of Mobile Gun Detachments i.e. 30 each to 12 Infantry Battalions. A copy of instructions regarding its use & for sick men.	

Army Form C. 2118

WAR DIARY
or
INTELLIGENCE SUMMARY.
(Erase heading not required.)

Place	Date	Hour	Summary of Events and Information	Remarks and references to Appendices
Gournay	27 Aug 15		M.L.M. M.L.E. 1014 Rifles arrived to day, issued to 5th, 6th, 7th & 8th Brigade Ammunition Columns; also 4 Companies A.S.C. 4th Divn Ammn Col. also 49 Bayonets to 1st, 4th Companies A.S.C. in exchange for those now in their possession.	Exh
do	28th	do	140 Rifles No.1, No.2, No.3 & No.4 L.E. arrived to day, bring the balance of rifles required to arm about 80 Units also 76 also employed at Divisional Head Quarters.III Officers Servants & grooms other than those of Officers serving with Cavalry, Engineers, Units of Infantry. III About 400 serving with Field Post Offices. The rifles issued are not light for heads III L.a. a Full. The 140 Rifles received were distributed to day.	Exh
do	29th	do	139 Rifles returned from above Units which take charts III L.a.a. were sent to the Base to day, all packed in chests rifle	

Army Form C.2118

WAR DIARY
or
INTELLIGENCE SUMMARY.
(Erase heading not required.)

Place	Date	Hour	Summary of Events and Information	Remarks and references to Appendices
Gosnay	30 Aug 15		200 Rifles were returned this day to Base in lieu of others issued not suitable to firing standard V.L.S.A. 160 Goggles auti-gas received viewed to Batteries as the rate of 30 per Battery. 50 Revolvers that received for trial as protection from hostile aircraft unable to pass over 25 per issue to the 140th Brigade, 1.25 to the 141st Brigade. Under authority of G.O.C. one Blanket per man is authorised to be drawn at once. Divisional Routine Order indents calling for Indents from Units. Instructions received that Sentries & Service Battalions are to be supplied with Badges of line battalions similarly for R.A., R.E., A.S.C. & R.A.M.C., the T.F. army others T.F. designation obtained & is to be used. In the case of Yeomanry Infantry not forming part of the line regiments where bad goods have to be provided R.A.6. will get them through T.F.B. as has that the T & Y trimming will not be issued.	Ets

Army Form C. 2118

WAR DIARY
or
INTELLIGENCE SUMMARY.
(Erase heading not required.)

Place	Date	Hour	Summary of Events and Information	Remarks and references to Appendices
Gouy	30 Aug/15		O.O. Base wires that a German Converted Machine Gun No 2193 will be sent up to 6 of 15th Battalion in lieu of Side Plate demanded for a Maxim Machine Gun Converted, none at present available.	
do	31 Aug/15		329 Rifles for firing blank VII S.a.a. returned to the Base on withdrawal from A.6.6. Kompanie etc. German Machine Gun Converted No 2193 received issued to the 15th Battalion. One Vermorel Sprayer & 300 smoke helmets issued to day for the purpose of carrying out a demonstration tomorrow in the employment & use of gas in our gas attack. Received instructions & amended list of Officers who should wear Amulet badge. Amulets should be plain bar no 1577 & row or bear any distinctive numbers thereon. D.a.D.O.S under the orders to not to wear an Amulets any longer.	EN/B

E.N. Buckland Major
D.a.D.O.S. 5th Div.

31/8/15

121/6971

47th Division

DADOS. 47th Division

Sept. 15

Army Form C. 2118.

WAR DIARY
INTELLIGENCE SUMMARY.
(Erase heading not required.)

Confidential

War Diary of
D.A.D.O.S.
47th Division
(Major Buckland
a.d.o.s)

1-9-15
to
30-9-15

[Stamp: A.B. OFFICE AT THE BASE — 4 OCT 1915]

55.   D.A.D.O.S. 47th Division

WAR DIARY
or
INTELLIGENCE SUMMARY. From 1st to 30th September 1915

Army Form C. 2118

Place	Date	Hour	Summary of Events and Information	Remarks and references to Appendices
Gonay	1st Sep 1915		200 Rifles in chests were sent to Railhead for despatch to the Base, these having been received from various ASC Units on being rearmed with rifles re-sighted for charger loading. Purchased at "Rogeo" French Stretchers for use in Trenches. Note held as French stores. Issued to 140th Brigade. Purchased 95 old motor tyres in call of 3 inch rope for muffling 35 G.S. wagon wheels for carrying out a special task. Had difficulty in purchasing some 200 odd more are required if obtainable. 4th Bn Royal Welsh Fusiliers posted to Division as a Pioneer Battalion without indent.	
do	2nd Sep do		39 Rifles in chests sent to Base today on receipt from various units on being rearmed with rifles re-sighted for VII Lat auf. 90 more old motor tyres purchased for carrying scheme above mentioned these being procured at Bethune. In the afternoon went to Lillers to arrange for purchase of 1/2 more motor tyres	

Army Form C. 2118

WAR DIARY
or
INTELLIGENCE SUMMARY.
(Erase heading not required.)

Place	Date	Hour	Summary of Events and Information	Remarks and references to Appendices
Goenay	3rd Sept 1915		58 Rifles despatched to the Base today on receipt from Units after being named with rifles not sighted for Mk VII La a. Head Quarters of Division moved today from Goenay to Drouvin.	
			On arrival at Drouvin, 15th Division had not reached position allotted for Depot, the cause of delay move to be further delayed by two lorries breaking down & very heavy rain. So no work completed except for transfer of Smoke Helmet Respirators which will be done tomorrow. The Depot at Goenay has in the School also an Office. Depot at Drouvin is in some farm Sheds & Office in a small School room in the Mairie.	
Drouvin 4th Sep 15			10u 20 8f 15 auto gas arrived tissued, the complete 24 per Battery. Of 990 Stabbing weapons arrived from Base Vare for issue to Grenadier Companies, 330 each for 140th, 141st & 142nd Brigades issued this day.	FB

Army Form C. 2118

WAR DIARY or INTELLIGENCE SUMMARY

Army Form C. 21

Place	Date	Hour	Summary of Events and Information	Remarks and references to Appendices
Drouvin	4 Sep 15		1 Experimental Traversing machine gun mounting (made in A.O.D. Base workshops) arrived. Instructions regarding it received yet. 250 canvas buckets for trench use purchased at Jeanville. 500 blankets received by 4th & 5th (?) & 6th Field Ambulances in lieu of feather waggons. Returning waggons were telegraphed for. 2 Lorries that broke down were replaced today & the Smoke helmets & Respirators removed from Journay.	
do	5 do		Traversing machine Gun mounting issued for trial & repair to 142nd Brigade. Field Artillery Order today authorises & "Rogers" trench telescope for company & per Squadron.	
do	6 do		1 Davon Super Telescope received. Issued to O.C. R.A. 26 Rogers patent trench sketchers purchased. Issued to 142nd Brigade. Ordered 158 more with local extension from to complete the 13 Battalion in Division.	EA

2353 Wt. W2544/1454 700,000 5/15 D. D. & L. A.D.S.S./Forms/C. 2118.

WAR DIARY
or
INTELLIGENCE SUMMARY.

Army Form C. 2118

Place	Date	Hour	Summary of Events and Information	Remarks and references to Appendices
Drawer	6 Sept 15		Label to complete establishment of 4th Royal Welsh Fusiliers as a Pioneer Battalion was sent to Base last night.	
do	7th	do	Blankets arrived as a first issue to Division of one per man 14,600. The route lorries have to take Railhead is fully 16 miles distant from Depot, so refilling point of 13 Reserve Supply each way to cope with this. 3 lorries where obtained on loan from Div Supply Column. Train was cleared (6 Trucks) before I gave but had lorries was not loaded until 10.45 pm the last had delivered to 120th Battalion at 12.45 am 6/9/1915. Delivery of blankets to 2 Infantry Brigade was made direct from Railhead, the 3rd Brigade being in the trenches although hard up, did not remove neither did many of the battalions. Some 6000 remained at Depot. 527 Bludgeons arrived from 4th Corps for issue to	

Army Form C. 2118

WAR DIARY
or
INTELLIGENCE SUMMARY.
(Erase heading not required.)

Place	Date	Hour	Summary of Events and Information	Remarks and references to Appendices
Drawing	8th Sep 1915	11.100	to Grenadier Companies issued equally to the 3 Infantry Brigades 9367 "Smoke helmets" tube pattern arrived from D.D.o.S. of Army late in the afternoon. Blankets arrived to-day the complete issue of one per man to whole of Division including units attached. Units who still have to draw are + Envelope shaped Helmets arrived for issue to each Batln. One of Ra- 9367 Smoke helmets received yesterday were issued to-day. Bludgeons also issued. Units not removing stores as regularly as desired got a Divisional order instated to urge removal daily The Boots repaired in D.V Shoemaking Shop during the month of August were as under:- Soles & Heeled 1924. Condemned & destroyed 923.	

Army Form C. 2118

WAR DIARY
or
INTELLIGENCE SUMMARY.
(Erase heading not required.)

Place	Date	Hour	Summary of Events and Information	Remarks and references to Appendices
Dranoutre	8 Sep 1915		The work carried out in the Divisional Laundry was as under during the month of August:–	

Received from Units duty

		Condemned	Washed & Repaired	Issued to Units
Shirts	30,669	1,943	28,726	31,275
Drawers	9,060	717	8,343	8,811
Vests	1,001	242	759	1,446
Socks	30,807	5,026	25,781	22,650
Totals	71,537	7,928	63,609	64,182

The work performed in the Tailors Shop was as under during the month of August:–

Articles	Number
Jackets & Dress	325 } Repaired
Trousers	330 }

160 D.C. Medal ribbon brooches made 4700 Grenadier badges made up.

Army Form C. 21

WAR DIARY
or
INTELLIGENCE SUMMARY.
(Erase heading not required.)

Place	Date	Hour	Summary of Events and Information	Remarks and references to Appendices
Drouvin	4 Sept 15		2/75 Blankets arrived to day to complete the issue of 1 per man in the Division. 600 Bomb Carriers received on purchase locally at Sheerville, these are to carry 10 Bombs suitable for carrying when the "Batty's" pitcher or Nos 5, 6, 7 Service pattern hand grenades. The Carriers previously in use were for carrying 5 grenades only. These are for use with the 3 Brigade, 2nd Ech. 2/3 Smoke Helmets tube pattern arrived from D.A.D.O.S. 1st Army	
do	16th	do	49 tents b.B.L specially authorised for issue to Signal Company, Head Quarter Staff, who are at present in bivouacs, arrived + were issued.	
do	17th	do	200 Gallons of oil for oil arguns dust in front of muzzle of guns when fired unfairly removed, this was purchased of French officially, sent to Divisny same night	

Army Form C. 2118

WAR DIARY
or
INTELLIGENCE SUMMARY.
(Erase heading not required.)

Place	Date	Hour	Summary of Events and Information	Remarks and references to Appendices
Drouvin	12 Sep/15		12 Short rifles fitted with Telescope sights for issue to Sharp-shooters arrived & were issued, 4 each to 140th, 141st & 142nd Brigades. 158 "Rogers" patent French Stretchers purchased & issued to the 3 Brigades, this completes the issue of 4 per Coy or 16 per battalion.	
do	13	do	50 Layers Stores allowed the Division for the purpose of boiling water Demand submitted. 1000 Tube helmets arrived from Aire, sent for them by lorry. O/C 20th Battalion returned 2 Smoke helmets, the pattern one had no tube fitted, the other was deficient of the rubber portion of the valve. Reported to D.D.S. 1st Army & had a Divisional Routine Order inserted for C.O.'s to have an immediate inspection to rectify existence of any Similar cases.	

63.

Army Form C. 21

Instructions regarding War Diaries and Intelligence Summaries are contained in F. S. Regs., Part II. and the Staff Manual respectively. Title pages will be prepared in manuscript.

WAR DIARY
or
INTELLIGENCE SUMMARY.
(Erase heading not required.)

Place	Date	Hour	Summary of Events and Information	Remarks and references to Appendices
Drouvin	14 Sep/15		D.D.S. 1st Army inspected Depot	
do	15th	do	Nothing important to record	
do	16th	do	do	
do	17th	do	Railhead changed from Lillers to Bacourt to day.	
do	18th	do	2000 Smoke Helmets, tube pattern, issued to Troops. Units on receipt of tube pattern smoke helmets are now returning the second ordinary smoke helmets on their charge, on receipt those are scanned, the serviceable ones are sent to	F.B

2353 Wt. W 2544/1454 700,000 5/15 D.D.&L. A.D.S.S./Forms/C. 2118.

64.

Army Form C. 2118

WAR DIARY
or
INTELLIGENCE SUMMARY.
(Erase heading not required.)

Place	Date	Hour	Summary of Events and Information	Remarks and references to Appendices
Drouin	18 Sep/15		The O.O. 1st Army Troops for reissue to other units, those found to be unserviceable i.e. with damaged eyepieces are sent to Abbeville for repair. The dipping 2323 were sent to O.O. 1st Army Troops & to Abbeville to day. Paymaster acknowledged having lost Imprest Account for month of August, asked for a duplicate copy also for duplicate copies of tradesmens receipts. Spent 5 hours to day obtaining duplicate receipts, total unfinished. Rather a slow [illegible] from letters to [illegible]	
do	19th	do	Sent to Aire for 1000 Lum le Roknets tube pattern. A bicycle urgently required for use with Head Qrs Ra. was purchased & taken direct to L.O.C. Ra at Lebribis. Instructions received to abolish Divisional Shoemakers shop on representation of Brigade Commanders from 21st Sept/15. Still obtaining duplicate receipts for lost Imprest Account.	

WAR DIARY
or
INTELLIGENCE SUMMARY.
(Erase heading not required.)

Army Form C. 2118

Place	Date	Hour	Summary of Events and Information	Remarks and references to Appendices
Rouen	20 Sep 1915		3000 Satchels for Smoke Helmets received. 3000 grenade fuse to be finished for placing in various positions in the front line. After much difficulty succeeded in purchasing 73 glass grenade fuse to be finished for placing in various positions in the front line. Took stock of Shoemakers shop P. Divisional shop only closed as far as Infantry Battalions are concerned. Out of 3 Shoemakers 25 were returned to the Battalions V 6 retained to keep the Divisional shop running for units other than Infantry, 12 Shoemakers tool bags one to each Regiment were returned 15 Regiments tall leather had V & E tops etc were equally divided taken back to Battalions to reopen Regimental Shops. V. He had left unprepared workshops were also divided between Regiments for an initial start. Receiver of Reformators 16,500 sent to Base, no longer required. 4698 also received from units as they are in possession of too much Kharki. 3149 sent to Base, 500 condemned & the balance of 1049 is now in for annotation.	EB

WAR DIARY
or
INTELLIGENCE SUMMARY

Army Form C. 2118

Place	Date	Hour	Summary of Events and Information	Remarks and references to Appendices
Drouvin	21 Sep 1915		Sent a lorry to Aire to draw 1000 Lunch Kebab tube futzes. Sent a lorry to Armentieres to draw 10 Grenade rods from 2nd Army Workshops. Purchased 200 gallons of oil at Auchel for G.O.C. R.A. for the purpose of allaying dust in front of muzzles of guns. Oil was sent up direct to R.A. at Lebechu after dark. 4 Telescope rifles for sharpshooters arrived. These were issued to 142nd Brigade as to where at same time sent for R.A. 93 Grenade fire extinguishers sent up to 1st Royal Welch Fusiliers at Lebechu, to dozen tape to 1/3rd Company R.E. also at Lebechu, at same time as oil for R.A.	
do	22 Sep 15		3 Abneyclocks arrived by motor car with bord. bails at 2am. Ye from Abbeville these were issued, 1 each to 140th, 141st & 142nd Bdes. for use with machine guns for indirect firing.	

WAR DIARY or INTELLIGENCE SUMMARY

Army Form C. 21

Place	Date	Hour	Summary of Events and Information	Remarks and references to Appendices
Drouvin	22nd July/15		Purchased 6 Fire Extinguishers from Boot Factory at Lillers & sent them up to 1/3 Coy R.E. after dark for use in Observation Posts etc. Ordered 16 French Carts at Lillers & Boulogne for issue to 4th & 5th French Mortar Batteries & sent 15 pairs up to 112st with 3rd London Battery, Condemned for receiver servicing.	
do	23rd	do	Purchased another 200 Gallons of oil for alloying Quartz in front of Guns & sent it up to 6 Batteries at Lebeche after dark. Purchase 6 Bicycles for use with the Slaughter Group of Guns for communication purposes, these were sent to Batteries along with oil. Went to Lillers re Purchase through delivery of French Carts. to Bucklow Circular issued & 6 copies received & issued to 140th & 141st Bde. do 22nd.	

WAR DIARY
or
INTELLIGENCE SUMMARY

Army Form C. 2118

Place	Date	Hour	Summary of Events and Information	Remarks and references to Appendices
Drouvin	24th Sep 1915		Moved Depot from Drouvin village to the Chateau roads by Divisional Head Quarters, this was done under difficulties of heavy rain. Head Qrs of Division moved forward to same location. Very heavy consignment of stores received from Base.	
do	25th	do	Wired all Brigades Nos. 1 R.E. pointing out that 1st Corps operations that all stores should be immediately withdrawn in view of actors. Wired for all Quartermasters to meet us at 11 a.m, all responded & discussed the question of keeping in touch with us & removing stores daily in the event of a move forward. Only at Sauwe Ne. lorries spoke on phone directing us to be prepared to move to Sauwe Ne lorries at 2.30 pm. Nearly all units removed stores by 5 pm. Commenced to move Depot at 5 pm, the fact long to last broke down within 50 yards of Depot. Looking of moving Stores	

Army Form C. 2118

WAR DIARY
or
INTELLIGENCE SUMMARY

(Erase heading not required.)

Place	Date	Hour	Summary of Events and Information	Remarks and references to Appendices
Drouvin	25 Sep 15		Was greatly impeded due to the bad quality of Troops the moving forward. The last lorry did not arrive in the route until 2 am. Smoke Helmets P.H. Rifle Grenades etc. were left at the Mairie for the time being.	
Sauchy-Lestrees	26 Sep 15		Sent a considerable quantity of stores out to units by lorry to San Pierre Vlaax Depot. Brought up from Drouvin three fourths of the Reserve of Smoke Helmets ordinary pattern by 10 pm. Sent up to Advanced Head Quarters for distribution to the 3 Infantry Brigade 3000 Smoke Helmets ordinary pattern. At 10 pm took up in Car Vermorel Sprayers (allowance Head Quarters at Sobesko) for distribution to 3 Brigade. Also Both Handcuffs. Placed in open arrest for absence from	Ends

WAR DIARY
or
INTELLIGENCE SUMMARY.

Army Form C. 2118

Place	Date	Hour	Summary of Events and Information	Remarks and references to Appendices
Saens-Hodoires	26.9.15		Went to Iberville & arranged for manufacture of 20 10 feet water troughs	
do	27	do	Railhead moved from Choques to Isbergue. Completed removal of Reserve of Smoke Shells from Graviers. Sent out a large quantity of stores to various units. Went to Lillers with D.A.D.O.S. 1st Corps to inspect French Carts. 35 Selous for a string B.C. arrived. Private Baislejohn J. joined from Base to complete Establishment	
do	28	do	Sent to D.A.D.O.S. 2nd Division at Locon, for F] Vermorel Sprayers. Went to Iberville & purchased 24 Canvas troughs for watering horses & 500 metres of rope also 24 "Rogers" French Stretchers. Instructed F] Gun N° 1205 both 13th London Battery burst reported to D.A.D.O.S.N.V.A.Q. & Railed for Kinfauch for dispatch to the Base. Same g.c. was also rendered unserviceable.	

Army Form C. 2118

WAR DIARY
or
INTELLIGENCE SUMMARY
(Erase heading not required.)

Place	Date	Hour	Summary of Events and Information	Remarks and references to Appendices
Locre lesbure	28 Sep 15		Sent up to Advanced Head Quarters Brigade 5000 Smoke Helmets by lorry also 35 Selous Breathing sets. Issued 150 Smoke Helmets to 4th Battalion Grenadier Guards as an urgent case as Units representatives could not find D.A.D.O.S. Depot of Guards Division. As an urgent case issued stores to Naval Armoured Car Section. Acting Sub-Conductor A. Harding by order of Col. of "J" Division was reverted to his permanent rank of Sergeant for an offence of "Absence from 1.30 pm 26th to 4-45 pm 26th Sept 1915 when important operations were in progress."	Sgd
do	do	do	Drafts of 520 men for Division arrived about 11 am and them each 2 Smoke Helmets each as they marched past Depot. 20,000 old pairs of Socks arrived & distributed by lorry to last time & to escort Units	Sgd

2353 Wt. W2544/1454 700,000 5/15 D.D.& L. A.D.S.S./Forms/C. 2118.

Army Form C. 2118

WAR DIARY
or
INTELLIGENCE SUMMARY.
(Erase heading not required.)

Place	Date	Hour	Summary of Events and Information	Remarks and references to Appendices
Sarcus-Lahoussoye	29th Sep/15		1000 Scabbing loops received from 4 Corps Relating to R.E.'s. These were issued to Head Quarters 61st Howitzer Brigade R.F.A. as they were very badly wanted. Brigade not attached to Division. Gun 15 pr No 1125 left Railhead for Base.	
do	30th	do	Sudden Orders received to move back to Goonay.	
Goonay	30th	do	Moved camp and all stores with the exception of Rector Supple left. Found Goonay occupied by 3rd Cavalry Division & absolutely no accommodation, formed Depot on road side near school. Damaged Gun No 1207 Barnings left Railhead for Base.	

F.H. Buckland Major
D.A.D.S.
4th Division

30 Sept 1915

12/7493

S.O.A.A. 47th Dinner.

Dec '15

Vol VIII

CONFIDENTIAL

Army Form C. 211

WAR DIARY
or
INTELLIGENCE SUMMARY.
(Erase heading not required.)

D.A.D.O.S.
47th Division
From 1st October to 31st October 1915

Place	Date	Hour	Summary of Events and Information	Remarks and references to Appendices
Gorney	1st Oct 15		Railhead moved from Focue Les-Mines to Chocques the morning. Busy day in the evening when 3rd Cavalry Division left this area was able to get accommodation in the open shed for use as a depot for stores & for cleaned off road side. Went to Chocque & saw a large quantity of rifles etc that had been picked up off battlefield. Large quantities of all kinds have already been dealt with & sent to Base. All known movements having been taken from Railhead.	
do	2nd	do	Indents to 16,601 new comers in Y by 11 from all ideals from Infantry Battalion Rd. have received for Equipment technical stores, the remainder to complete establishment these were sent off to Base same morning & also Buck items specially telegraphed for with an explanatory confidential letter to D.O.S. Base	

Army Form C. 2118

WAR DIARY
or
INTELLIGENCE SUMMARY.
(Erase heading not required.)

Place	Date	Hour	Summary of Events and Information	Remarks and references to Appendices
Gosnay	2nd Oct 15		Interviewed all Battalion Quarter Masters Urged the necessity of getting demands in early. Thes Brigade came out of trenches this morning. I. A. D. R. Offr. worked for all single Inducts used in action to be returned to me for despatch to Abeville for re-impregnation. All routes allowance of under clothing demanded & clothing lodge for drill.	
do	3rd do		To Raickhead. Observed & herewere Re-bures & collected large quantities of (a.b) equipment to meet incidents. As not ready knew. Oh could be obtained a lorry was sent to several Hospital Bearing Stations in the afternoon & a large quantity was obtained in this way but still not sufficient. It is hoped to complete at Raickhead tomorrow. It has been discovered that are somewhat rearming their men with Lhars Rifles. a Dij. Order has been issued tonight calling upon OC's Infantry Battalions to render	

WAR DIARY
or
INTELLIGENCE SUMMARY.
(Erase heading not required.)

Army Form C. 211

Place	Date	Hour	Summary of Events and Information	Remarks and references to Appendices
Gonay	3rd Oct 15		a return showing the number of Rifles long & Bayonets, short & long Bayonets in their possession & (b) The number of Short rifles & Long Bayonets in their possession. An adjustment will be made in due course on receipt of reports. Had a Divisional order noted directing any captured German Machine guns to be sent to us for record & dispatch to the Base. Brich stores required to repl. Division again wired for.	
do	4th Oct 15		Secured remainder of accoutrements to complete in detail from various Convg. Hospital. German Machine Gun No 2854 captured by Division orders was sent to Base in Truck 12/247. Gulf Large quantities of Stores demanded were wired for again.	

WAR DIARY or INTELLIGENCE SUMMARY

Army Form C. 2118

Place	Date	Hour	Summary of Events and Information	Remarks and references to Appendices
Lozay	5 Oct 1915		On account of matter did not for accoutrements demand by line had to be sent to Base as nothing canvas be obtained from Railheads. 2 German machine guns captured by Division were sent to Railhead for despatch to the Base in Truck No 42116. The Regd. Nos. of Guns were No 2487/2508.	46
Sotteville les Rouen	6 Oct 15		Left Lozay at 10 am for Noeux-les-Mines all stores were brought up as well as Reserve of Gumboots Whole by 2.30 pm. Office & Store are situated in a house in the main Bethune Noeux les Mines road opposite Brewery, accommodation as regards both very bad. Upon, no cover for others now except for a couple of small rail covers awaiting issue to Units. Railhead moved from Choques to Noeux les Mines	

WAR DIARY
or
INTELLIGENCE SUMMARY.

Army Form C. 211

Place	Date	Hour	Summary of Events and Information	Remarks and references to Appendices
Loos-en-Gohelle	6th Oct 15		Trucks delayed enroute & 6 arrived today, busy day clearing. has as most units are on the Spot this was done quicker than expected.	
do	7th	do	Conductor A. Balne, arrived to replace Sergt Harding ordered to Base on reversion from acting Sub-Conductor. 100 foot Observation Ladder received from 4th Corps issued to S.O.B. R.a. Defects now in demand out to Base for 37½ Rifle long 534 Bayonets Scabbards in place Stars rifles & bayonets in possession of units See memo[?] note on the 3.10.15	
do	8th	do	9 Telescope Rifles that received Viewed to Brigades 3 each. 50 Cartridges for Salvo apparatus received from 4th Corps issued to same found at 4th Corps. 39 Syringes received from 4th Corps in lieu of Vermorel Sprays	

Army Form C. 2118

WAR DIARY
or
INTELLIGENCE SUMMARY.
(Erase heading not required.)

Instructions regarding War Diaries and Intelligence Summaries are contained in F. S. Regs., Part II and the Staff Manual respectively. Title pages will be prepared in manuscript.

Place	Date	Hour	Summary of Events and Information	Remarks and references to Appendices
Secunderabad	9th Oct 15		15 Pistols .45 inch arrived, issued to the 3 Brigade Staff	
do	10th	do	Scrap dealing having handed over to Conductor Roberts left for the Base today	
do	11th	do	Nothing special to record	
do	12th	do	4 butters iron for rifles received for trial, 6 given to 140th; 6 to 144th; 15 to the 142nd R.R.c. Reported on as Excellent.	
do	13th	do	Nothing special to record	

Army Form C. 2118.

WAR DIARY
or
INTELLIGENCE SUMMARY.
(Erase heading not required.)

Instructions regarding War Diaries and Intelligence Summaries are contained in F. S. Regs., Part II. and the Staff Manual respectively. Title pages will be prepared in manuscript.

Place	Date	Hour	Summary of Events and Information	Remarks and references to Appendices
Nieuwkapelle	15th Oct 1915		95 Inspirescopes received at the rate of 8 per Battalion balance to complete are still due. The 100 foot Observation Ladder issued to 2/6th having been unfavourably reported upon, no immediate opportunity of testing its back & time taken to assemble it was returned to me & she was sent to Railhead direct for despatch to the Base.	1/9
do	do			
Nieuwkapelle	15th Oct 15		Left Steenvoorde - les- Skries at 10 am with all stores except Reserve Smoke helmets. Lorries went back to Railhead & brought up todays receipts. Same accommodation nil beyond a 2nd Coy. Details housed in grounds of Villa Arnold under the three Offices in Villa.	
Nieuwkapelle	16th	do	Reserve Smoke helmets brought up today from A.S. Skins got here under cover of fire via Small Coors	SB

WAR DIARY
or
INTELLIGENCE SUMMARY.

(Erase heading not required.)

Army Form C. 2118

Place	Date	Hour	Summary of Events and Information	Remarks and references to Appendices
			The 35 Salvos breathing set were examined to day by the Expert representative & were entirely defective & rejected & 2 others ready to these were returned with representative to Corps for recharging.	
Mazagabs	17 Oct 15		Sne to hi hut like battery be the only battery eventually to be used had D.R. Order issued to the effect stating Gun Entails complete all back to 2 p for Officers Men. 100 Staff Relieh arrived viewed men of 140 & 141 R.F.A. in trenches for trial. 100 Dragoes arrived viewed & issued to Same Brigade (note?)	
do	18th	do	Arms and to be withdrawn from all Puschi's Sketches Cairo. Div: Orders issued directing O.C.'s to return arms to the above for despatch to Base. Private bottles arrived in replacement of the little declared	

Army Form C. 21

WAR DIARY
or
INTELLIGENCE SUMMARY.
(Erase heading not required.)

81

Place	Date	Hour	Summary of Events and Information	Remarks and references to Appendices
Mazargues	19th Dec 15		Lieut Brazier arrived & issued to Division Scheme to notify Nos 5,14 & 16 Field Ambulances arrived from 4th Corps for their dues. Depôts moved from under trees at villa arranged to some small stables in Mazargues. Brewery close at hand. Both balances shifted to hospital.	
do	20	do	Lieutenants Holyard & St Laurence arrived for duty, in replacement of Lieuts. Addison & Penn, transferred to No 1 & 2 A.D. workshops 3rd Corps. Both balances evacuated from hospital, Pt: la o.r. much too old for the appointment of Brigade harness officer, reported same to D.D.O.S. Many lathes & a grinder to be sent at once. As O.C. Grease now owns a Divisional Routine Order was published directing Units to bring their own cans or other receptacles to receive the oil & grease.	F.W.S.

Army Form C. 2118

82

WAR DIARY
or
INTELLIGENCE SUMMARY.

(Erase heading not required.)

Place	Date	Hour	Summary of Events and Information	Remarks and references to Appendices
Mazingarbe	2nd Oct 15		15 Pistols illuminating & holders arrived 6 day & issued to 140th; 141st & 142nd Bdes, the complete issue of 10 Field to each Brigade. 10 Trench Carts obtained from Ordnance, these will be issued to French Mortar Battery as soon as faults have been rectified daily from Base. Privates Fenn & Allison despatched to No. 1 & 2 A.O.D. Workshops 3 Bays respectively for duty. On returning etc sent to & from on 16th were The Saline breathing respectively for duty, returned today, after being recharged.	
Mazingarbe	3rd Oct 15		577 Long Rifles & 541 Short Bayonets arrived from Base Issued to all Regiments of 140th; 141st & 142nd Brigades. Horse Shoes quite fit for further use are being returned to the Base, a Div. Order was issued directing COs to ensure the necessity of economy, as expenditure of Shoes is very large & great difficulties are experienced in obtaining adequate supplies. FAB	

2353 Wt. W2544/1454 700,000 5/15 D. D. & L.   A.D.S.S./Forms/C. 2118.

WAR DIARY
or
INTELLIGENCE SUMMARY.

Army Form C. 21

Place	Date	Hour	Summary of Events and Information	Remarks and references to Appendices
Mazingarbe	23 Oct/15		Interviewed D.A.D.O.S. of Division at bulk clothing store taking over his supplies. Signalling Panniers for issue to Battle of Battalions of the Division. Balance of all bulk clothing demanded in bulk after excluding amounts asked for individuals already sent to Base	
do	24 Oct/15		100 Braziers arrived & issued	
do	25th	do	Nothing special to report.	
do	26th	do	Orders of D.O.G. 10 Blud grans were issued to 10th Division for trial by Brigade 10 Trench boots issued 5 each to 141st and 142nd Brigade Mortar Batteries 85 Thomas Lagers received, 13 were issued, 10 Each Battalion for trial to report.	

Place	Date	Hour	Summary of Events and Information	Remarks and references to Appendices
Nasriyeh	26 Oct 15		Divisional Routine Order issued a fatiguing out Rifles that was being manufactured without cut off & without long range sights may be issued to troops on G.H.Q. approval, but mounted troops must have rifles fitted with cut offs.	
do	27	20	4 Telescopic Rifle Sights received, 2 each to 40 & 41st Brigades 10 telescope sketches received to each issued to 76th F Amb. On Ranas Weekly fatiguing out has now ceased. Oil will be applied to butts, to prevent jamming or failure of machine gun firing the. A.O. all ranks are forbidden to clean any rifle at and time "without first removing the bolt & magazine of the rifle."	

Army Form C. 2118.

WAR DIARY
or
INTELLIGENCE SUMMARY.
(Erase heading not required.)

Place	Date	Hour	Summary of Events and Information	Remarks and references to Appendices
Sanyanghi	28th Oct 15		Divisional Routine Orders mention calling attention to Div. R.O. No. 492 of 25th July 1915 pointing out the fact that "It must be clearly understood that the Sale by Company seale for the purpose of issuing abandoned Government property is not a medium of getting rid of surplus property in the possession of Units. Recently, for example, one surplus rifle & the Salvage Company, as if they were salvaged material. The practice is to be discontinued at once. Surplus stores are in future to be returned through the authorised channels only."	
			Woollen Vests. Sizes to be demanded by Units	
do	29th Oct 15		125 Tents E.P. arrived & issued to Units on a given distribution for Ourks accommodation of the Troops.	

WAR DIARY
or
INTELLIGENCE SUMMARY.

(Erase heading not required.)

Army Form C. 2118.

Place	Date	Hour	Summary of Events and Information	Remarks and references to Appendices
Morlancourt	29 Oct 15	1000	Gum boots, thigh pattern, received & distributed. 5 Inch bath purchased & issued to the 110th Brigade Trench Mortar Battery. A Divisional Routine Order inserted to the effect that "Every effort is to be made to continue from day to day until completion, the Salvage of Arms, ammunition, stores, clothing &c. Commanding Officers will insure that every party, however small, brings out such quantity as they can carry. They will hold Officers, N.C.Os & men in charge of returning parties responsible that this is carried out."	
do	30	do	Some winter clothing received & issued. A Divisional Routine Order inserted to the effect that Steel helmets are to be dealt with as Trench Stores within the Division & handed over from Brigade to Brigade as relief take place in the trenches. When the Division goes into Reserve the Steel helmets will be retained.	

Army Form C. 2118

WAR DIARY
or
INTELLIGENCE SUMMARY.
(Erase heading not required.)

Place	Date	Hour	Summary of Events and Information	Remarks and references to Appendices
Nasiriyeh	2nd Oct/15		A Div. R. Orders issued directing that all Great Coats replaced by Coats, sheepskin-lined, are to be returned to the Ordnance & filling point at once for despatch to Basra.	
			Drawing attention to the urgent necessity for the immediate return to the Base of all surplus rifles due to casualties or other causes.	
do			The work done in Laundry during the month of Oct/15 has been as under:— Shirts 14,564; Drawers 5416; Vests 1914; Sundries 563 Clothing washed :— do 22,020; do 15,460; do 11,336; Sodo 1168 & B.Belts 1705 Clothing issued :— do 20,720; do 11,379; do 3,133; — do 1372 Received from Units Sindi :— do 1,564; do 604; do 198; Sundries 617 Condemned :— In addition to above 168 Jackets 20, 26 Trousers; 128 Great Coats & 25 Pataloons were cleaned & issued to Tailors shop for repair.	Sd.

2353 Wt. W2544/1454 700,000 5/15 D.D.&L. A.D.S.S./Forms/C. 2118.

WAR DIARY
or
INTELLIGENCE SUMMARY.

Army Form C. 211

Place	Date	Hour	Summary of Events and Information	Remarks and references to Appendices
Shazmgarh	3rd Oct 19.15		The work done in Tailor shop was 6/10 pairs Jackets 2.D 164; Trousers 167; Great Coats 196 & Pantaloons 44. The position at present occupied by Depôt is less far the most advanced one close to Divisional Head Quarters Lines up with the Guns. The detachment living in huts at for some time at Shazmgarh, but we have shifted them along with the stores. The health of the detachment is very good.	Sd/-

5 Nov 19.15

F.A. Buckland Major
D.A.D.O.S.
47 Division

12/7637

WAR DIARY
INTELLIGENCE SUMMARY

Army Form C. 2118

D.A.D.O.S, 47th Division
From 1st Novr. 1915 to 30th Novr. 1915

Place	Date	Hour	Summary of Events and Information	Remarks and references to Appendices
Mazingarbe	1st/10/15		7 Railway Trucks containing 45 tons of Clothing, boots, Rugs have arrived since arrived. Such a large consignment caused a good deal of shock but was successfully coped with rapidly and in spite of heavy rains & view from limited accommodation.	
do	2nd	do	2 Trucks containing 12 tons of Clothing Rugs have & Detail stores arrived. Following on yesterdays large consignment rather congested things, but that drawing early soon relieved the situation. An allotment of 400 x Gum boots thigh pattern having been made to the Division, will upon receipt be distributed as under:- 3 Brigade as 1000 each; Pioneer Battalion 300; Divisional Artillery 420; Engineers 220; Troops Signal Company 40 v R.A.D. 6. 20 a Divisional R. officer was inserted to the effect	

WAR DIARY or INTELLIGENCE SUMMARY

Army Form C. 2118

Place	Date	Hour	Summary of Events and Information	Remarks and references to Appendices
Mazingarbe	2nd/10/15		The Gun boots are to be treated as Brigade stores & Commanders of Infantry Brigades, Divisional Artillery & that above named units naturally & equipment & special inspections are made every week, to ensure they the boots are being fairly used for legitimate purpose & to guard against loss. Reports are to be rendered by Brigade Commanders, on the 1st of each month to me, giving accurate information of the number of pairs that have become unserviceable, every pair of which is to be returned. The boots are to be used solely by men of Brigade Units while actually employed in the trenches & gun emplacements only.	
do	3rd	do	Discussed with a. a. & q. b. g.l. the advantage & dis- advantages of opening a Divisional Armourers Shop in view of a reduction of Armourers in Division, decided in favour of a Div Armrs Shop. A/Sergt Stanley of Re Dwyer arrived	

Army Form C. 2118

WAR DIARY
or
INTELLIGENCE SUMMARY.
(Erase heading not required.)

Place	Date	Hour	Summary of Events and Information	Remarks and references to Appendices
Mazingarbe	4th 10/15		On receipt with G.O.C. R.A. the question of dealing with the receipt of 18 pr Guns & Equipment & the return to Base of the 15 pr Guns & Equipment now with 2 R.F.A. Brigade in Division. All arrangement fully made.	
do	5th	do	Information received that 18 pr Guns & Equipment above with the assistance of one portable ramp & one small forward ramp. The last vehicle one off loaded at 9.15 p.m. The Station yard was clear of the whole of Equipment & the last vehicle left yard at 10.5 p.m. The new Equipment was handed to the units in an open space near the Station. The 15 pr Guns were taken out of action same night, arrived at Source le Comte at 12 m.p. & parked along with the 15 pr Equipment for the night under an R.A. Guard.	

WAR DIARY
or
INTELLIGENCE SUMMARY.
(Erase heading not required.)

Army Form C. 2118

Place	Date	Hour	Summary of Events and Information	Remarks and references to Appendices
Magnyla Fosse	5/Nov/15		The Equipment detrained was as follows:-	
			Advance QF. 18 pounder Carriages — 18	
			Limbers QF. 18pr. Carriages — 18	
			" " Wagon Ammunition — 54	
			Wagons Ammunition QF.18pr — 54	
do	do	do	After making arrangements with LofC Rs and RTOfficer Scenic-Ardoines the train for entraining the 15pr Guns & Equipment was run into position at 2.45pm in place of 2pm as arranged with French authorities. Entraining commenced sharp at 2.45pm and two portable ramps, the last vehicle was put aboard at 4.50pm.	
			The Equipment entrained was:-	
			Advance BR. 15pr. Guns 9; Carriage 10; Limbers 12; Wagons Ammunition 24; Limbers 24 Carriage 28.6.	
			Only 3 Guns were returned in place of 12 & 10 as	

WAR DIARY
or
INTELLIGENCE SUMMARY

Army Form C. 2118

Place	Date	Hour	Summary of Events and Information	Remarks and references to Appendices
Bazinghen	6 Nov 1915		1 Gun & Carriage are due (to 14th Battery & 2 Guns & Carriage to 13th Battery R.F.A. of the 5th Brigade R.F.A. As 14th Brigade Equipment arrived, it was only possible to withdraw one Brigade at a time for tactical reasons, so all 3 Brigades are in action & Guns can only be withdrawn as nights. The other half of 18 pr Equipment is due to arrive on the 10th when it is intended to build out another Brigade of 15 pr (6th Brigade) & the third (II nd Brigade (1st) on the 13th Nov 1915.	
do	do		On the 5th Divisional Routine Orders were inserted regarding Jackets for carrying Ammunition. Helmets will only be supplied to Units as demanded as it is found that most Units have the old Jackets from Jackets & few them on the new Jackets also, drawing attention to French & Belgian Boys wearing complete suits of khaki & Some Case, the Commdg Off directs to see the practice is discontinued.	

Place	Date	Hour	Summary of Events and Information	Remarks and references to Appendices
Mazgarhi	6 Nov 15		12&8 Boots Gum thigh & Yeo F.S. arrived & leaves to authorized for frames, a busy day indeed. A Divisional R. Order walks to the effect that no civilian labour to be employed in boot repairing shops. Furnishes A.A. Rtns with a list of the principal artches of Clothing & Equipment issued to the units of Division from date of landing in the Country 16th March to 31st October 1915 so that a comparison can be made with both the monthly lists of issues made. This has been done with a view to checking excessive issues & for A.A. Rtns to take any action considered necessary.	
do	9th	do	Two Lewis Machine Guns returned by Divisional Army were asked to be sent to Ruhlen a/c depot to the Base. They were both damaged particularly No 487 & incomplete. They of the second one was 863. Such IO 2085a left Marseilles Rueghouse ck on 5th Nov 1901. (6) Land reports to J.A.G. req. q^a yet	

WAR DIARY
or
INTELLIGENCE SUMMARY.

(Erase heading not required.)

Army Form C. 2118.

Place	Date	Hour	Summary of Events and Information	Remarks and references to Appendices
Mazingarbe	10th Nov 9/15	15.00	Nurs Rose arrived from Base & day charged to Div: but turned out to be for 15th Division. Nurse handed over to S of Do. Truck No. 20858 still missing. Base & Rly Station wired to ascertain cause of delay. Went to Ambulance train & asked to interview the D.A.D.S. 1st Division regarding taking over office & department prior to the Division going back into Corps Reserve. Sent 32 Bearers to 1st Bde & 40 Bde at Fort Glatz ₁ members.	
do	11th	do	Truck No. 20858 arrived with Nurse Rose the day after taking 6 days to arrive. In view of Division moving back into Reserve on the 15th declared question with Brigade bearer Rs of receiving balance of 15pr Equipment & dispatch of 15pr Equipment to the Base as Railhead will this move from Sousa-les-Mines to Lillers. It is intended to go to Lillers tomorrow to interview R.T.O. & select depot to hand guns the day after detraining	

Army Form C. 2118

WAR DIARY
or
INTELLIGENCE SUMMARY.
(Erase heading not required.)

Place	Date	Hour	Summary of Events and Information	Remarks and references to Appendices
Mayur-Sultan	21/10/15		Went to Moudros lashores to interview D.A.D.O.S. etc. re landing & taking over Stores the on Division & getting its Reserve. From Moudros, went on to Tellero with Staff Captain R.A. to arrange for reception of 15" Equipment arriving with 15". R.G.A. said the Guns he could not be detained as Tellero as other training of Troop prevented it. Base wired asking if Equipment could be received on 15". Lacs G.O.C. R.A. who for date back to 14" on account of Division moving into Reserve. Base informed. Base again wired saying 32 Inch had already been loaded in Truck & difficult to obtain & Lord the could not be accepted on the 15" so arranged Consuls Head Quarters at home Stationery R.A. at 10 p.m. who agreed to receive Bases & D.D.O.S. 1st Army informed. Divisional Routine Ordr. issued & drawing attention to General R. Ord. 1257. regarding Special winter clothing & when issued when withdrawn & disposal of defining public clothing.	

WAR DIARY
or
INTELLIGENCE SUMMARY.

Army Form C. 2118

Place	Date	Hour	Summary of Events and Information	Remarks and references to Appendices
Mazingarbe	13/10/15		Went to Marles-les-Mines to discuss questions with D.A.D.O.S. of Division who in exchange wants such as Pants, Soyers stoves, Guns Boots, Braziers etc to Line transport. 50 Trench stick helmets received. D.A.D.O.S wired today 18/pr Gun Equipts. Could not be sent to Neuve Chapelle but Illesmeis 4th Corp instructions.	
do	14th	do	Bres wired saying 36 Truck containing Brigade La Hait of 18/pr Gun & Equipment that night & would arrive 15th. 18/pr Equipment in Traffic Berthin wired saying 15/pr Equipment in 36 Truck arrived at Acwis-le-Bouers at 2 pm today. Arranged with G.O.R.A & R.T.O for reception. No news of train at 2 pm; at 5 pm Traffic out & train would arrive at 7 pm. booking parties therefore dismissed till 7 pm. No train at 7 pm & did not arrive until 10.10 pm. Detraining took place at 10.15 pm Each Spar table ramp that vehicle was detrained at 2.45 am on 15th Nov 15. all being parked in a field near Railhead.	14-19-1915

Place	Date	Hour	Summary of Events and Information	Remarks and references to Appendices
Mozufferpore	14/10/15		As no Cranes of any description were available, some considerable difficulty was experienced in detraining and to the fact that some trucks were but loading & some side loading, thus making the job a slow & hard one, under the circumstances the work was done in very good time. Equipment detailed thus far on to RFA consisted of 15pr Guns - 16; Carriages 18; Limbers 18; Wagons Ammunition Gr & Limbers 34. At present the 15pr Guns of 6th & 9th Brigades RFA are all in action but it is proposed to withdraw them on the night of 15/16th & 16th/17th Oct 1915 and them at Sewriee lo–boire Station all of two Brigades Equipment to Base on Wednesday arranged with Q.O.6 R.A. & R.T.O. have been made accordingly. In view of more to narrow Gauche lines & Lorry loads of Stores etc. to new Depot, the whole Retrieval in Reserve will bent there on the 13th inst	EB

Place	Date	Hour	Summary of Events and Information	Remarks and references to Appendices
Marbel Thiele -to-Mine	15 Nov 1915		Reported to D.D.O.S. 4 Army at 3.30 am the receipt Landing one of 18pr Guns & Equipment to the 6th & 7th Brigade R.F.A. on arriving back at Hazebrouck. Railhead moved from Steenwerck to Lillers. Division completed move back into Reserve to-day. Transferred from Hazebrouck to Ablain St Office to double-houses. Divisional Routine Order issued re new pattern Grenadier Badge with Scarlet flame.	
do	16 Nov 15		Went to Steenwerck to arrange with R.T.O. &c. returning two Brigades of 15pr Guns & Equipment tomorrow. R.T.O. was uncertain as to whether train could be obtained R.T.O. wired at 10 pm saying entraining could be taken in hand at 9 am tomorrow. Wired G.O.C. R.A. Canadians Cooking party &c 2nd Army to Hazebrouck to & 2nd Army looked up for 12 Rifle Grenade reel	SG

WAR DIARY or INTELLIGENCE SUMMARY

Army Form C. 2118

Place	Date	Hour	Summary of Events and Information	Remarks and references to Appendices
Meteren Morbecque	17 Nov 1915		Lt. Col. Monks reshore Sharp at 8.30 am for Meteren - to shine to witness entraining of 15th Equipment of 6th Bde at Le Rota for despatch to the Base. Entraining commenced at 9.15 pm & finished at 3.30 am 18th Nov 1915. Vehicles obtained were Gun 16 Carriages 24; Limbers 24; Wagon Ammunition 54 Limbers 54; 12 Wagons G.S. should also have gone to make Equipment complete 6 however were retained. Issued & complete establishment of the Divisional Ammunition Column the remaining 6 have also been retained 3 temporarily & 3 for issue to the Brigade Machine Gun Companies now being formed.)	
Morbecque	18 Nov 1915		Instructions received regarding demand Aug 9 of 48 Machine Guns & Equipment for the 3 Brigade Machine Gun Companies and instructions to each Brigade to deliver them personally with demand to furnish demands by telegram today as early as possible. 6 Trenchboats received from Lombardie	₤B

101

Army Form C. 2118

WAR DIARY
or
INTELLIGENCE SUMMARY.

(Erase heading not required.)

Place	Date	Hour	Summary of Events and Information	Remarks and references to Appendices
Nables Newbries	19/10/15		Demanded 48 Lewis Machine Guns; 10 lagons G.S. limbered; 3 Carts water; 3 Carts bread; 3 lagons G.S. for equipping the 3 Brigade Machine Gun Companies. 4 Machine Guns were also demanded for "Rebel Raids"	
do	20	"	3 "Webb" Bomb Throwers obtained from O.O. & Corps & issued one each to 140th, 141st & 142nd Brigades.	
do	21	"	Machine Gun bacon t 6665 arrived for 2nd Battalion, to replace a damaged one sent to base. Leather Jerkins except for those immediately likely to leave the trenches are to be withdrawn, the few Units affected directed by letter to return at once.	
do	22nd	"	Nothing of importance to record	S.B.

2353 Wt. W2544/1454 700,000 5/15 D. D. & L. A.D.S.S./Forms/C. 2118.

WAR DIARY
or
INTELLIGENCE SUMMARY.
(Erase heading not required.)

Army Form C. 2118.

Place	Date	Hour	Summary of Events and Information	Remarks and references to Appendices
Hardelot-les-bains	23rd/10/15		48 Colne Machine Guns arrived Havre & back to the 12 Battalion	
			6 French hats received from Contractor	
			1800 Leather Jerkins arrived from Base thewards Infantry.	
do	24th	do	3300 Blankets received from Paris, being first consignment to meet second blankets per man. Issued to 102 Infantry Brigade direct from Railhead, the Brigade being billetted in vicinity of Railhead Lillers.	
			Base notified this balance of blankets will be sent up at the rate of 1000 per day until demand is complete	
			4 Carro Machine Guns for Royal Welsh Fusiliers arrived Havre	
			Discussed question of Divisional Ammunition Shop	
			A.A.G. Hughes ast draft copy of instructions	
			Acting Lieb. Col. Mc Quinn left for Woolwich via Lillers & Havre under instructions by telegram from O.i/c Records 3rd Echelon, Base. D.B.

2353 Wt. W 2544/1454 700,000 5/15 D. D. & L. A.D.S.S/Forms/C. 2118.

Place	Date	Hour	Summary of Events and Information	Remarks and references to Appendices
Hinges	25 Nov 15		Sent one Vermorel Sprayer to the A.D.M.S. & 200 Tube Batteries and 6 Lebels to Gnl Divisional Laboratories for a special demonstration & examination of gas and of the gas masks used under the Gas Expert. Spent most of morning looking for a suitable Divisional Armourer Shop & about to be fixed up & will no doubt finally decide on one in Busnes. The General Officer Comdg announces to the Division with much satisfaction that the Comdr-in-Chief yesterday inspected the 142nd Infantry Brigade as representing the 47th (London) Division, for the purpose of congratulating it on its achievements at the Battle of Loos. Sir John French expressed his highest appreciation of the "magnificent work done by the Division" during the fighting & stated in most emphatic terms his full confidence that the Division would not fail to gain further laurels during the war.	

Army Form C. 2118

WAR DIARY
or
INTELLIGENCE SUMMARY.
(Erase heading not required.)

Place	Date	Hour	Summary of Events and Information	Remarks and references to Appendices
Issued at Duxbwa	4th Nov/15		Blankets & hats arrived & issued to various units	
do	do		D.D. & S. Army B. Cholen Smith inspected departl Office. The usual question of securing all R.F.a. Brigade with Repro: deficiencies of vehicles with Brigade and Divisional Ammunition columns under new A.T.S.G. 1098's received &c. Issued Divisional Route Orders re leaving trenches flannel shirts in lieu of under vests due from Base that available. Rifles to be examined & gauged by Armourers due to large number of misfires apparently caused by the distance of the bolt from end of the chamber being occasion during to wear. Any rifles found unserviceable beyond repair by Armourers to be demanded by units immediately, and, Instructions re landing works of Armg of Armourers Shop to be opened on do 5th Octobr/15 after inspection of all rifles have been carried out. Only two came in action, one will be repaid at Roven Y 10 Oct One of Staff Columns for 2 others Sergt. W. Ryan joined Division in replacement to S. Cord. Quinn transfero Woolwich. A.B.	

2353 Wt.W2544/1459 700,000 5/15 D.D.&L? A.D.S.S./Forms/C.2118.

Army Form C. 2118
WAR DIARY
or
INTELLIGENCE SUMMARY.
(Erase heading not required.)

Place	Date	Hour	Summary of Events and Information	Remarks and references to Appendices
Boulogne	18/10/15		580 Jerkins & Fur Coats issued to Units entry into the Trenches were received & issued to other Units who are liable.	
			Issued Routine Order re all Gum Boots &c. &c. which are not serviceable tanned (or retained) at the front, must be returned to Ordnance Depots for dispatch to the Base whatever may be their condition and	
			Timber must not be purchased locally over £5 in value when such is done a certificate must be obtained from the Contractor showing the origin from which the timber was obtained. This is necessary to prevent the importation of timber from abroad into the Army areas.	
			Went to Abbeville re canvas & to settle an account. 1850 Blankets arrived towards issue of 2 per man. Two Lorries still away under repair.	

Army Form C. 2118

WAR DIARY
or
INTELLIGENCE SUMMARY.
(Erase heading not required.)

Place	Date	Hour	Summary of Events and Information	Remarks and references to Appendices
Souluz Trenches	29 Nov 15		490 Blankets received (conditions of 2 per man). Demanded additional tools for use of Armourer on Divisional Armourer Shop (to be opened on the 5th Dec 1915).	
do	30th	do	6 Telescope Rifles received issued to 19th Battalion Nos 52856 & 76854. Nos 6541; 5697; 5541 & 5489 to 20th Battalion. Health of detachment very good	

F.A. Buckland Major
D.a.D.o.S.
9th Div

1/12/15

DADBS 47th An. / Doc. / Vol IX

CONFIDENTIAL WAR DIARY D.A.D.O.S. 47th Division

INTELLIGENCE SUMMARY From 1st December to 31st Dec 1915

Army Form C. 2118.

Place	Date	Hour	Summary of Events and Information	Remarks and references to Appendices
Noulette-les-Mines	1st Dec 1915		4 Maxim Guns returned by 1st Royal Welsh Fusiliers. Having been used with Lewis Guns. Relisted Nos 10664; 10000; 5818 & 9290. Deep check to base via Lillers Railhead. 400 Blankets arrived. Lieut A.T. Thread A.O.D. joined for instructions under D.A.D.O.S. Division proceeded on a Divisional Tactical march to —	
do	2nd	do	Division returned from Route march as above. Lieut. went to Busnes in the evening to 140th Brigade with two Gauges for the purpose of examining Canying Out an inspection as a safeguard against misfires. Gauges .0645".074 to be passed on to 140th & 141st Brigade for same purpose	

Army Form C. 2118.

WAR DIARY
or
INTELLIGENCE SUMMARY.
(Erase heading not required.)

Place	Date	Hour	Summary of Events and Information	Remarks and references to Appendices
Marles les-Mines	3rd Dec 6/15		10 Loyers Stoves arrived from Base	
do	4th	do		
do	5th	do	2400 Sandbags & 300 pickets &c. arrived returned to the Base without removal from Railhead under orders from Base, this is due to sufficient hand being received to equip all liable for immediate entry into the trenches above having been despatched from Base after reporting sufficient in hand. Also the Armourer at Divisional Dep at Busheres arranged for to working of Lap L. Laurele billetting, Ratoning & Sanges Services tools to arrive to run the Shop were demanded on the 29.11.1915.	

Army Form C. 2118.

WAR DIARY
or
INTELLIGENCE SUMMARY.

(Erase heading not required.)

Place	Date	Hour	Summary of Events and Information	Remarks and references to Appendices
Sailly-Labourse	6 Feb 1916		Nothing unusual occurred	
do	7th		do	
do	8th		do	
do	9th	"	Went to Laventie-les-Thines to interview D.A.D.o.S. 1st Div re taking over his depot. Also a Division going back into the trenches about the 15th instant. D.A.D.o.S. not present but received Despatch 25 Lewis Stove arrived to complete 50 allowed to Division	[sig]

WAR DIARY or INTELLIGENCE SUMMARY

Army Form C. 2118.

Place	Date	Hour	Summary of Events and Information	Remarks and references to Appendices
Sailly-la-Bourse	10th Dec 15		350 Steel Helmets arrived & 175 each issued to 141st & 142nd Bdes.	
do	11th		Nothing of importance to record	
do	12th		do	
do	13th		do	
do	14th		Received telegraphic instructions to proceed to Calais 15th then cancelled & proceed to Noeuilly on the 16th	
do	15th		Railhead moved to Noeux-les-Mines from Lillers. Detrained in the line again. Office moved from Sailly-la-Bourse & Depot from Auchel to Noeux-les-Mines	

Army Form C. 2118.

WAR DIARY
or
INTELLIGENCE SUMMARY.
(Erase heading not required.)

Place	Date	Hour	Summary of Events and Information	Remarks and references to Appendices
Marseilles	15th Dec 15		DDoS 1st Army interviewed me at Charles-le-hure prior to my departure tomorrow for Marseilles	
Marseilles	do		Arrived at 2.3 pm, visited Depot Office & received with Lieut Shead, to whom all Office records have been handed over to on his assuming the duties of DaDoS. EH	
	16 Dec 1915			F.A. Buckland Major DaDoS 47th Divn
do	do		Interviews G.O.C. 47th Division & taking over duties of DaDoS from Major Buckland	
do	16 Dec		Major Buckland left for duty as ODO Marseilles. Arrangements Headquarters Officer Jows also to be cleared. Permits were issued. Regulations Sanitary Section to Claw Asports & refuse from precincts of Depot	

2353 Wt W2544/1454 700,000 5/15 D. D. & L. A.D.S.S./Forms/C. 2118.

Army Form C. 2118.

WAR DIARY
or
INTELLIGENCE SUMMARY.
(Erase heading not required.)

Instructions regarding War Diaries and Intelligence Summaries are contained in F. S. Regs., Part II. and the Staff Manual respectively. Title pages will be prepared in manuscript.

Place	Date	Hour	Summary of Events and Information	Remarks and references to Appendices
Kantara on the Nile	17 Dec		Separate Brigade Ward Officers arrangements to Brigade to to distribution animals to Base Warrant Officer continues notices of taking animals for new Brigade time	
do	18 Dec		15 Wagons G.S. received and driven to 47th D.A.C. to complete equipment. Pte Stretton evacuated to the Base.	
do	19 Dec		Nothing unusual occurred.	
do	20 Dec		Pte Williams transferred to 3rd res C.S. for duty.	
do	21 "		Nothing unusual occurred	
do	22 "		do	

Army Form C. 2118.

WAR DIARY
or
INTELLIGENCE SUMMARY.
(Erase heading not required.)

Instructions regarding War Diaries and Intelligence Summaries are contained in F. S. Regs., Part II. and the Staff Manual respectively. Title pages will be prepared in manuscript.

Place	Date	Hour	Summary of Events and Information	Remarks and references to Appendices
India Co-two	23 Dec		Special Trench Stores received Tubs Washing, Latrine Buckets, Brayers etc	
do	24		Demanded Lewis Guns to replace Maxims & Vickers on charge 1/3 g 1/4 London Regiments 1 18 pdr Gun to replace one Bulgarian for 18th Bty R.F.A.	
do	25		Water procured normally	
do	26		Demanded 1500 Tubes Smoke Helmets vide GHQ D5 6/115 26/9/38 of 22/9/15	
do	27		Transport very unsatisfactory. I interviewed O.C. DSC this line not being sufficient. Word from ADOS. Corps 1 Gun & Carriage received for 18th London Bty to replace one "U"	

Army Form C. 2118.

WAR DIARY
or
INTELLIGENCE SUMMARY.
(Erase heading not required.)

Instructions regarding War Diaries and Intelligence Summaries are contained in F. S. Regs., Part II. and the Staff Manual respectively. Title pages will be prepared in manuscript.

Place	Date	Hour	Summary of Events and Information	Remarks and references to Appendices
Marles les Mines	28 Dec		Nothing unusual occurred	
do	29	"	Heavy receipt from Base	
do	30	"	do.	
do	31	"	5000 Socks arrived for Divisional Reserve.	

A.B.Shaw
Lt
DADOS
47 Div

Rans 0347 Div
Jan
Vol I

WAR DIARY
or
INTELLIGENCE SUMMARY

Army Form C. 2118.

DADOS 47th Division
Army July 1st 1916 to Jan 31st/16

Place	Date	Hour	Summary of Events and Information	Remarks and references to Appendices
Noeux les mines	Jan 1	1	Nothing unusual occurred	
do	"	2	Lewis Guns arrived for 1/3 & 1/4 London Rgts. Pte Cox 7509 reported for duty	
do	"	3	Pte Anderson to 8 Div for duty. New Trench Stores received from Base. Pte Latham reported for duty from 15th Div.	
do	"	4	Trench Stores issued to 140. Bde.	
do	"	5	ditto 141. Bde.	
do	"	6	250 Bayonets issued to 140 & 141 Bdes & Div Artillery. Opened up new Record Place for Smoke Helmets etc	

WAR DIARY
or
INTELLIGENCE SUMMARY.

(Erase heading not required.)

Army Form C. 2118.

Place	Date	Hour	Summary of Events and Information	Remarks and references to Appendices
Nœux les Mines	1916 Jan 7		Headquarters moved from Vaurecourt to Nœux les Mines	
do	8		Extra Trench Stores delivered	
do	9		Transferred Reserve to new store	
do	10		4 Trench Mortars to 10q Workshop for Repairs	
do	11		Nothing unusual occurred	
do	12		464 Gun Butts Mag^s to 142 Bow	
do	19		8 4.5" Howitzers & 48 limbers received from Base in exchange for 5" Gun Equipment	
do	20		Return of 5 in Howitzer Equipment to Base.	

Army Form C. 2118.

WAR DIARY
or
INTELLIGENCE SUMMARY.
(Erase heading not required.)

Place	Date	Hour	Summary of Events and Information	Remarks and references to Appendices
Vieux Berquin	Jan 27		1 Vickers Machine Gun arrived for 140 Bde Machine Gun Co in lieu of Colt returned.	
do	" 28		ditto	
do	" 29	11-30 A.M.	Not a 4.5 Howitzer out of action. Demanded from Base — for 8th How Bde	
		6 west Spring Back Howrs demanded & received from Corps Reserve, same day to 140 & 141st Bde.	
do	" 31		4.5 Howitzer received from Base for 8th How Bde. of which Deficing Parts "Yellow" Returns 12 & 2 p.m.	
			Nothing further occurred during the month of January other than above mentioned	

F.G.S. Evans
Lt
Adj.
27th Division

War Diary.

Capt. A. J. Schaan. D.A.D.S. 47th Division.

From February 1st — 29th 1916.

Vol XI

Army Form C. 2118.

WAR DIARY
or
INTELLIGENCE SUMMARY.
(Erase heading not required.)

Da Dos 47th Divison
From Feb 1st to Feb 29th 1916

Place	Date	Hour	Summary of Events and Information	Remarks and references to Appendices
Nocux les Mines	Feb 1.		Machine Gun Team arrived & issued to 142 Machine G. Coy	
"	2		Nothing unusual occurred	
"	3		14,000 P.H. Tube Helmets from 4th Corps.	
"	4		Above distributed under instructions from 4 Corps BHQs. Team Conductor returns and returned to Base. Gun Boat Expert reported for Duty	
"	5		Inspection of Offrs & Stores by Col Hone AA & QMG Br. Prior to this departure.	
"	6		Acid Sinks for Machine Gunners from 4 Corps Shop & issued same day.	
"	7		Gun Boat Expert Lecturer to Div Shoemakers	

Army Form C. 2118.

WAR DIARY
or
INTELLIGENCE SUMMARY.
(Erase heading not required.)

Place	Date	Hour	Summary of Events and Information	Remarks and references to Appendices
Scene des Iunc	Feb 8	8	"B" Batty 176 Bde R.F.A attached to Division & posted to 6 8th Monty Bde.	
"	"	9	3rd & 4th London Rgts Bgd Divisions for 56th Division.	
"	"	10		
"	"	11	Nothing unusual occurred.	
"	"	12		
"	"	13	Gas Alarm.	
"	"	14	D.D. O.S. 1st Army — inspection of Office & Stores	
"	"	16	Division moved to Corps Reserve at Lillers.	

Army Form C. 2118.

WAR DIARY
or
INTELLIGENCE SUMMARY.

(Erase heading not required.)

Instructions regarding War Diaries and Intelligence Summaries are contained in F. S. Regs., Part II and the Staff Manual respectively. Title pages will be prepared in manuscript.

Place	Date	Hour	Summary of Events and Information	Remarks and references to Appendices
Lillers	Feb 28		Leave Gun drivers for 8th Batts howitzer Regt — demanded on night of 26th inst. Otherwise General workshop nothing unusual occurred on except left flank.	

10/3/16.

A.S.Warren
Capt. D.A.D.O.S.
47th Divn.

Davos 4y Dw
Vol XII

Confidential 47th Division
D.A.D.O.S. Detail
N.S. Khan Capt.

WAR DIARY or INTELLIGENCE SUMMARY

Army Form C. 2118.

From 1—3 1916.

Place	Date	Hour	Summary of Events and Information	Remarks and references to Appendices
Lillers	1916		"Sub-Conductor Ryan Bols N.O. 140 Bow rejd for 1st Army for duty.	
Bruay	9		Division moved to Bruay.	
"	11		4 2" Trench Mortars arrived for formation of 7th T.M. Battery from II Corps.	
"	13		1000 Divis Smoke Helmets were received and issued.	
"	14		Visited 23rd Division re Trench Stores 4 Trench Mortars were issued to 7th T.M. Battery on formation	

Army Form C. 2118.

WAR DIARY
or
INTELLIGENCE SUMMARY.
(Erase heading not required.)

Place	Date	Hour	Summary of Events and Information	Remarks and references to Appendices
Bruay	May 15		Recon Stores to Fresnicourt.	
Loos & Bouvin	" 16		Office Stores to Mine's Bouvin.	
"	" 17		Office transference to Stores at Fresnicourt.	
Fresnicourt	" 20		Office transference to Mairie Fresnicourt.	
"	" 21		Indoor Showers & Ammonia Shops to Fresnicourt.	
"	" 22		Issue of Recreus P.H. Helmets to Officers & men.	
"	" 24		G.O.C. Inspection Depot etc.	

Army Form C. 2118.

WAR DIARY
or
INTELLIGENCE SUMMARY.
(Erase heading not required.)

Instructions regarding War Diaries and Intelligence Summaries are contained in F. S. Regs., Part II. and the Staff Manual respectively. Title pages will be prepared in manuscript.

Place	Date	Hour	Summary of Events and Information	Remarks and references to Appendices
Grevillers	Mar 27		In reply to instructions A.O.C. detached men in accordance with instructions received from D.H.Q.	
"	28		Received Shells.	
"	29			
"	31		Received Shells. Other than firing nothing unusual occurred on days left blank.	

8/4/16.

J.S. Kray
Capt. DADOS
47th Division.

47

Davos 47 Dw

Vol XIII

A.Q.O. Detachment 47th Division
H.Q. Heavily [?]

WAR DIARY
or
INTELLIGENCE SUMMARY.
(Erase heading not required.)

From 1 – 30 April 1916.

Army Form C. 2118.

Place	Date 1916	Hour	Summary of Events and Information	Remarks and references to Appendices
[?]	General April		Railways shelled heavily	
"		6	D.D.O.S. 1st Army visited Office	
		8	Arrival of 8 Lewis Howitzers for L.M. Batteries	
		10	D.A.Q.M.G. visited Office	
		12	Detachment Musketry course	"
		13	"	"
		14	"	"
"		16	Enemy Aero reported at 10·15 pm two Zeppelins approaching	

Army Form C. 2118.

WAR DIARY
or
INTELLIGENCE SUMMARY.
(Erase heading not required.)

Place	Date	Hour	Summary of Events and Information	Remarks and references to Appendices
Evevia	April 28		Lieut-Colonel H Dean for duty.	
Cowl			Otto Hans ground routine nothing unusual occurred no change left flank	
	2/5/16			J.S.S. End Capt [signature] 10/7/16 Bom

Army Form C. 2118.

WAR DIARY
or
INTELLIGENCE SUMMARY
(Erase heading not required.)

A.O.D 47th Division
Capt. A.V. Kean D.A.D.S

From 1st May 1916 to 31st May 1916

Place	Date	Hour	Summary of Events and Information	Remarks and references to Appendices
France	May 1		1st to 8th nothing unusual to note.	
"	"	9	Coal & W Buffer Chief Clerks forwarded on leave and returned 17th May.	
"	"	10	Inspected B.A.C's and D.A.C. and found no surplus equipment.	
"	"	"	"C" Squadron K.E.H. and Cyclist Coy left Division	
"	"	11	Two Lewis Guns returned to Base - rec'd from K.E.H.	
"	"	14	One Lewis Gun demanded for B10th Regiment to replace one damaged by Shell fire.	
"	"	15	Despatches of Artillery ackd	
"	"	16	One Lewis Gun received and issued to 21st Lon Reg	

Army Form C. 2118.

WAR DIARY
or
INTELLIGENCE SUMMARY.
(Erase heading not required.)

125

Place	Date	Hour	Summary of Events and Information	Remarks and references to Appendices
Fricourt	Feb 18	12-3	S.O.S. Rockets received from Corps and issued as follows 8 to 141 Bde, 4 to 140 Bde.	
"	"	31	Two Lewis Guns demanded from Bgde for 7th and 8th London Regiment to replace those knocked.	
"	"	22	Six Vickers Guns demanded to replace six Vickers lost in enemy attack — for 140 Bde M.G. Coy.	
"	"		Lieut Denison A.O.D reported for Instructions in D.O.O's duties	
"	"		S.O.S lens can receive 11.5 p.m. Detachment p/Coop to turn out to chambers 11.55 p.m.	

Army Form C. 2118.

130

WAR DIARY
or
INTELLIGENCE SUMMARY.
(Erase heading not required.)

Place	Date	Hour	Summary of Events and Information	Remarks and references to Appendices
Trenchard	May 23		Two Lewis Guns received and delivered to 7th & 8th Ln. Regiments	
"	"		Six Vickers Guns received and delivered to 140th Bde M.G. Coy. Two from receipt of demand to handing over Guns 30 hours.	
"	"		Two Vickers Guns demanded for 141 Bde M.G. Coy to replace casualties	
"	24		Six Lewis Guns demanded to replace casualties in 7th & 8th London Regiments.	
"	"		Six 3 in Stokes Motars demanded for 140 Bde to replace others twin.	
"	25		Two Vickers Machine Guns received and handed over to 141 Bde M.G. Coy.	

Army Form C. 2118.

WAR DIARY
or
INTELLIGENCE SUMMARY.
(Erase heading not required.)

Place	Date	Hour	Summary of Events and Information	Remarks and references to Appendices
Greenwood	May 26		Office and Depot moved to Bruay.	
"	"		Six Lewis Guns received and issued; three cases to 1/D 9/8th London Regt.	
"	"		Six 3" Stokes Mortars recd and issued to 140 Bde.	
"	"		D.D.O.S. First Army called.	
Bruay	27		2 – Q.F. 18 pdr Guns condemned by I.O.M. Lenters Section.	
"	"		Armourers Tailors & Shoemakers moved to Bruay.	
"	28		1 Limber Gun cases for A 236 Battery. Two Lewis Guns exchanged for 20th Lon Regt to replace lost.	
"	30		2- Q.F. 18 pdr Guns returned to 341st Battery R.F.A.	

Army Form C. 2118.

WAR DIARY
or
INTELLIGENCE SUMMARY.
(Erase heading not required.)

Place	Date	Hour	Summary of Events and Information	Remarks and references to Appendices
Bruay	May 29		1 Lewis gun issued to "A" 236 Battery.	
"	"	30	Two Lewis Guns issued to 20th Regt.	
"	"	30	Four Lewis Guns demanded for 22nd Lincs Regt to replace lost and damaged by them. Visited Div Hd Qrs with Capt R O'Schinny DAQMG.	
"	"	31	Sub-Cond. Aylett granted one month's leave on certain of France. Other than above mentioned nothing new to report.	

1/6/16

M. Smith
Capt
S.A.D.O.S.
47th Div.

133

Army Form C. 2118.

WAR DIARY
or
INTELLIGENCE SUMMARY
(Erase heading not required.)

A.O.D 91 Headquarters, 47th Divn.
Capt. A.T. Shean. D.A.D.O.S.

Vol 15

Place	Date	Hour	Summary of Events and Information	Remarks and references to Appendices
Bray	June 1st		Four Lewis Guns received and returns to Army Workshop returned to Div on adoption of B.A.C'd. 1 Cpl trans. 3 Wagons G.S. D.A.C. 20 Wagons G.S. Div 4 Wagons Limbers G.S.	
"	"	2	D.A.D.O.S. to 6 Army units to Bray and inspection carried out	
"	"		Indent submitted to Base for 3,800 Rifles S.M.L.E. to replace as condemn numbers of Rifles O.L.M.L.E.	
"	"	6	1900 Rifles S.M.L.E. received and review	
"	"	7.	1900 " " "	
"	"	13.	Armourer Sergeants Shoemakers &c moved to Bus on taking over from 23rd Division	

Army Form C. 2118.

WAR DIARY
or
INTELLIGENCE SUMMARY.
(Erase heading not required.)

Place	Date	Hour	Summary of Events and Information	Remarks and references to Appendices
Barlin	14 June		Offices and Stores to Barlin.	
"	15 "		Two 2" Trench Howitzers received and return to "Z" Battery	
"	18 "		D. a. D. O's returned from leave. 10gr40	
"	22 "		Lieut Demain left Division for temporary duty with R.N. Division.	
"	24 "		Transferred to Calais Base for ano & stores.	
"	25 "		One 2" Trench Howitzer demanded for "Y" Battery to replace one lost. One Carriage Q.F. 18 pdr demanded to replace one lost by shell fire for B 236 Battery. R.F.A.	
"	27 "		26 Lewis Guns demanded to complete Infy Battalions to 6 each	

Army Form C. 2118.

WAR DIARY
or
INTELLIGENCE SUMMARY.
(Erase heading not required.)

Instructions regarding War Diaries and Intelligence Summaries are contained in F. S. Regs., Part II. and the Staff Manual respectively. Title pages will be prepared in manuscript.

Place	Date	Hour	Summary of Events and Information	Remarks and references to Appendices
Barly	28 June		One 2" Trench Mortar returned of carrier to "Y" Battery. One Ammg's Q.F. 18 pdr received of carrier to B.236 Battery. R.F.A.	

7/7/16

Newman
Capt.
Indus
47th (London) Division.

Confidential

WAR DIARY
or
INTELLIGENCE SUMMARY

(Erase heading not required.)

Army Form C. 2118.

Headquarters
17th Division
Capt. A. T. Kead D.A.D.S.S.

Vol 16

Place	Date	Hour	Summary of Events and Information	Remarks and references to Appendices
Baslus	July 2		Two racing carriages demanded for 141 Machine Gun Co. One Lewis Gun demanded for 20th Regt	
"	4		Carriage F. Q.F. 18 Pdr. with dial sight demanded for B237 Batty to replace one hit by hostile shell fire. One Ord. Q.F. 18 Pdr. without breech fittings demanded for "C" 235 Battery to replace one hit by hostile shell fire	
"	5		26 Lewis Guns rec'd and issued — two to each Inf. Batt. to complete to establishment of 6 Lewis Guns per Batt. Two machine guns for 141 M.G. Co. demanded. One Lewis Gun carriage to 20th Kn. Regt.	
"	6		One 3" Stokes Mortar demanded for 146 Bde to replace one condemned.	
"	7		One Carriage Q.F. 18Pdr rec'd and issued to B 237 Batt. One Ord. Q.F. 18 Pdr received & issued to 235 Batty. 3 Vickers Guns demanded for 141 Bde Machine Gun Co. 1 Vickers Gun demanded for 140 M G Coy	

[13]

Army Form C. 2118.

WAR DIARY
or
INTELLIGENCE SUMMARY.
(Erase heading not required.)

Place	Date	Hour	Summary of Events and Information	Remarks and references to Appendices
Barly	July 9		One 3" Stokes Mortar recd & issued to 140 Bde.	
"	" 10		3 Vickers Guns recd & issued to 141 M.G. Coy.	
"	"		1 Vickers Gun recd & issued to 140 Bn. M.G. Coy.	
"	"		Brigade Q.M. Stores of arms dealt in 140 Brigade	
"	" 11		" " " " 142 "	
"	" 12		One Vickers Gun demanded for 140 M.G. Coy.	
"	"		One 3" Stokes Mortar ammunition for 142 T.M. Batty.	
"	"		Two 15 Pdr B.L.C. Guns limbered & ammunition Wagons	
"	"		recd & handed over to 47 Div Arty.	
"	" 13		Three 3" Stokes Mortars recd from O.O. IV Corps Insp / M.G. Coy.	
"	" 14		One Vickers Gun demanded for 141 Bde. M.G. Coy.	
"	"		One 3" Stokes Gun recd & issued to 142 T.M. Batty.	
"	" 15		One Vickers Gun demanded for 141 at M.G. Coy.	
"	"		3 — 3" Stokes issued to 140 Bde.	
"	" 16		One Vickers Gun issued to 141 M.G. Coy.	
"	" 17		Office & Stores removed to Coubelin L'Abbé	

138

Army Form C. 2118.

WAR DIARY
or
INTELLIGENCE SUMMARY.
(Erase heading not required.)

Place	Date	Hour	Summary of Events and Information	Remarks and references to Appendices
Bachlau L'Abbe	July 18		Armourers Tailors Boot makers shops moved to Canteen L'abbé.	
"	" 19		Two "B" Trench Mortar Ammunition for "Z" T.M. Batty	
"	" 21		Two " " " " " " " " " " "	
"	" 23		" " " " recd & issued to " " "	
"	" 24		One Vickers Gun demanded for 140 M.G. Coy received 26th	
"	" "		Three Vickers Guns demanded for 140 M.G. Coy received 29th	
"	" 28		Office Gens moved to War Cometer	
"	" 30		Office & all attached moved by train to Fleurs	

A.S. Reed
Capt DADOS
47th (London) Division

3/7/6

Army Form C. 2118.

WAR DIARY
INTELLIGENCE SUMMARY
(Erase heading not required)

Headquarters
47th Divn
Capt. A.F. Skeam, D.A.D.O.S.

Vol 17

Place	Date	Hour	Summary of Events and Information	Remarks and references to Appendices
Hors(?) de Train	Aug 1st		Offices and our stores moved by road to Hotken le Grand	
Friday	"	4	Moved to YVRENCH.	
"	"	6	One Vickers Gun returns to 141 Machine Gun Coy to replace one condemned.	
"	"	7	Instructions from D.Q.G.S. to complete 1st & 8th Bns Bats Lewis Battalion supplies with Distinguishing Marks.	
"	"	11	17 lorries of Bombing Brigades returns & to II Army from rear.	
"	"	"	Base changed from CALAIS to HAVRE.	
"	"	12	Fourteen Vickers Guns demanded to replace MAXIMS.	
"	"	"	Auty O.S.B. 1/2775/2 dt 29/7/16.	
"	"	15	Moved to St Riquier.	
ST RIQUIER			36 Lewis Guns and 14 Vickers received for Battalions and Machine Gun Coys	

A.D.S.S./Forms/C. 2118.

Army Form C. 2118.

WAR DIARY
or
INTELLIGENCE SUMMARY.
(Erase heading not required.)

Instructions regarding War Diaries and Intelligence Summaries are contained in F. S. Regs., Part II. and the Staff Manual respectively. Title pages will be prepared in manuscript.

Place	Date	Hour	Summary of Events and Information	Remarks and references to Appendices
St RIQUIER	Aug 18	72	Lewis Pack who had cart received and returned.	
"	"	20	Moved to VIGNACOURT.	
Vignacourt	" 22		Moved to FRESHENCOURT.	
Freshencourt	" 25		A.D.O.S. III Corps inspected Office and Stores and Shops.	
"	" 29		1 – 18 pdr Gun and Carriage received to C 237 Battery to replace one condemned.	
"	"		1 – 18 pdr Gun received to B 236 Batty to replace.	
"	"		1 – 18 pdr Carriage received to 31st Battery to replace.	

16/9/16

Stafford
Capt Davis
17th Divison

Army Form C. 2118.

WAR DIARY D.A.D.O.S. 17th Division
INTELLIGENCE SUMMARY.
(Erase heading not required.)

From 1st to 30th Sept 1916

A.J. Shaw Capt.

Vol /8

Place	Date	Hour	Summary of Events and Information	Remarks and references to Appendices
Fricourt	1916 1st			
"	6		One 18 pdr Gun arrives for B.235 Battery	
"	7		One Lewis Gun received for 15th London Regt.	
"	8		600 Rifles issued to Divisional Troops and reserves to Infantry Batt to Ord for reserves of Ammunition. One 4.5 Howitzer arrives for D 235 Battery	
"	9		16 Signalling Lamps made in Divl Armourers Shops and issued to Brigade HQrs and Battalions. Distinguishing letters and Strips issued to D.A.Q. B.HQrs and Battalions for Aeroplane Signalling. One 18 pdr Carriage arrives for A 235 Battery	
"	10		Moves to ALBERT.	

Army Form C. 2118.

147

WAR DIARY
or
INTELLIGENCE SUMMARY.
(Erase heading not required.)

Instructions regarding War Diaries and Intelligence Summaries are contained in F. S. Regs., Part II. and the Staff Manual respectively. Title pages will be prepared in manuscript.

Place	Date	Hour	Summary of Events and Information	Remarks and references to Appendices
ALBERT.	Sept 11/15		Ration ALBERT. Men Skilled heavily. Artillery supply park transferred.	
"	12	8P	Haircuts Lewis Guns received and issued same day.	
"	14		One 3" Stokes rotar for 142 T.M. Battery rec'd & issued	
"	16		Two Vickers Guns drawn for 1st H. M.G. Coy. Crated from Abbeville and delivered to unit immediately.	
"	17		One 18pdr armour for 34 Battery.	
"	23		9000 S.A.A. [?] received and issued to Infantry.	
"	20		Reliefs Division ad coming out of line and unit in rest area.	

2353 Wt. W2544/1454 700,000 5/15 D. D. & L. A.D.S.S./Forms/C. 2118.

Army Form C. 2118.

143

WAR DIARY
or
INTELLIGENCE SUMMARY.
(Erase heading not required.)

Place	Date	Hour	Summary of Events and Information	Remarks and references to Appendices
ALBERT	Sept 20 to		During period Sept 20th to 30th. Captured following guns etc detailed as received:- 4.5 Howitzs. 1. Guns Vickers. 8. 15pdr Guns. 6. " Lewis 30 Carriages 15pdr 4. " Stokes 3" 3	

A.J. Head
Capt
D.A.D.O.S.
17th Division

Confidential

WAR DIARY D.A.D.O.S.
or
INTELLIGENCE SUMMARY. 47th Division
B.E.F.

Army Form C. 2118.

Capt. A.J. Skead.

Place	Date	Hour	Summary of Events and Information	Remarks and references to Appendices
Albert	Oct 3		One 18 pdr Gun received for C/237 Battery. R.F.A.	
"	"		" " " " " C/236 " "	
"	"		One 4.5 How. received for D/235 Battery. "	
"	"		" " " Ammn Carriage for D 238 Bty	
"	7		Moved to FRICOURT.	
FRICOURT	8		Rather place.	
"	"	10	3 Lewis Guns received for 20th London Regiment	
"	"	"	2 Lewis Guns received for 17th London Regiment.	
"	"	"	1 Lewis Gun received for 19th London Regt.	
"	"		Moved to ALBERT.	
ALBERT	"	14	Moved to L'Etoile by road.	

Army Form C. 2118.

WAR DIARY
or
INTELLIGENCE SUMMARY.
(Erase heading not required.)

Place	Date	Hour	Summary of Events and Information	Remarks and references to Appendices
L'ETOILE	Oct 15		Entrained at PONT REMY, at 11.p.m. 19th Div Supply Column Lorries attached Ordnance of this Division left for duty with another Div.	
"	16		Detrained at GODEWAERSVELDE. BELGIUM. Lorries at 3 pm and proceeded by Road to Stores and Offices at RENINGHELST.	
RENINGHELST	16		Winter Clothing demands were made/drawn from D.O.B.	
"	18		Four Lewis Guns received for 19th London Regiment. Four 3-ton lorries from 5th (Australian) Supply Column reported for duty.	
"	19		One 15pdr Carriage received for B 235 Batty, R.F.A.	

Army Form C. 2118.

146

WAR DIARY
or
INTELLIGENCE SUMMARY.
(Erase heading not required.)

Place	Date	Hour	Summary of Events and Information	Remarks and references to Appendices
RENINGHELST.	Oct 20		One 18 pdr Carriage received for A 236 Battery R.F.A.	
"	"		Four Lewis Guns received for 8th London Regiment.	
"	"		Two " " " " 6th " "	
"	"		One " " " " 23rd " "	
"	"		523 Howitz Battery 237 Bde Joining Division.	
"	23		One 18 pdr Gun for C 237 Battery R.F.A.	
"	"		One Lewis Gun for 15th London Regt.	
"	"		One Lewis Gun " 7th " "	
"	23/24		Winter Clothing received and distributed.	
"	26.		Letter to A.D.O.S. X Corps asking for relief of 05777 L/Corpl. H. Beaumont now 1/23 Pte. J. Wickham.	

Army Form C. 2118.

WAR DIARY
or
INTELLIGENCE SUMMARY.
(Erase heading not required.)

Place	Date	Hour	Summary of Events and Information	Remarks and references to Appendices
RENINGHELST.	Oct 28		One 3" Trench mortar demanded for 141 T.M. Battery & received.	
"	"	30	One 18pdr Gun received for B 236 Battery	

A.J. Sheard
Capt Davis.
A/4th Division

Confidential

WAR DIARY
of D.A.D.O.S. 47th Division
Capt A T Shaw

November

INTELLIGENCE SUMMARY.
(Erase heading not required.)

Army Form C. 2118.

Vol 20

Place	Date	Hour	Summary of Events and Information	Remarks and references to Appendices
RENINGHELST	Nov 2		3" Stokes Mortars received for 141. Trench Mortar Battery.	
"	" 11		V/47 Heavy Trench Mortar Battery is now sent back to Base.	
"	12		3" Stokes mortars received for 140 Trench Mortar Battery.	
"	13		D.A.D.O.S. proceeded to England on leave and returned 24th inst.	
"	27		24 Lewis Machine Guns received from Base to complete Battalions to 10 guns each arm reserve. Other has also nothing of importance to report.	

16/
12/16.

T H Shaw
Capt.
D.A.D.O.S

Army Form C. 2118

WAR DIARY
or
INTELLIGENCE SUMMARY.
(Erase heading not required.)

2 A.D.O.S.
47th Division
Capt. A. H. Kemp

Place	Date	Hour	Summary of Events and Information	Remarks and references to Appendices
Renescure	Dec 1916	2	Lanshaw, Shadwell & Callas attached to that division as a Corps designs by D.A.D.O.S. acknowledged by decens dnyad report that the adopter have been	
			Army reminders to G.H.Q. ords QQ97/169/A/5 dates 29/11/16.	
		4	During attaching reorganises. Three Brigades now consists of four Brigades supplying - three to Bde. the following Cavalry Machine & Battns outside to one ammunition dump. etc	
		6	One Lewis & Vickers received for 142 Machine Gun Coy.	
		8	Opened by D.A.D.O.S. drawn shops onto the Q.O./164/15 dates 3/12/16. Not. Q.M.G. has at this All Gum-Shot Collars attached has been sent by the Commander-in-Chief, is considered to an essential item and it is recommended generally to all	

2353 Wt. W2544/1454 700,000 5/15 D.D. & L. A.D.S.S./Forms/C. 2118.

Army Form C. 2118.

WAR DIARY
or
INTELLIGENCE SUMMARY.
(Erase heading not required.)

Place	Date	Hour	Summary of Events and Information	Remarks and references to Appendices
Enghly	Dec 5 (cont)		Consolidate on position as approved	
"		14.	One 18 Pds Gun spares for A 335 Battery	
"		17.	One Lewis Gun received for 7th London Regiment. 34 Lewis Guns received, this leaves to add 4 only, but two required to twelve Lewis Guns for Battalion.	
"		23.	One Lewis Gun received for 18th London Regiment 8th "	
"		25.	One Vickers Gun received for 140 Machine Gun Coy. A Mes[?] and Stokes rods recd for 142 T.M. B[?]	
"		27.	10 Stokes recuper Fuses D.O.S. [illegible]	

Army Form C. 2118.

WAR DIARY
or
INTELLIGENCE SUMMARY.
(Erase heading not required.)

Place	Date	Hour	Summary of Events and Information	Remarks and references to Appendices
Roving Adv	Dec 31 (a.m)		Acknowledge receipt of Bath Stone etc conf circulars & instructions thereto.	
	"		Ack. recn. instructions for 7th Leins. Regmt.	
	"	5	Find L.B. Command orders not arranged. to be issued.	
	"	31	Ack. recpt. of recn. instructions & purposed visits to School of Instruction.	

16/1/17

Wilson
Capt.
for D.D.S.
17th Division

Army Form C. 2118.

WAR DIARY

Contents January DADOS.
1917 INTELLIGENCE SUMMARY 47th Division.
(Erase heading not required.) Capt. A.T. Skead.

Instructions regarding War Diaries and Intelligence
Summaries are contained in F. S. Regs., Part II.
and the Staff Manual respectively. Title pages
will be prepared in manuscript.

Place	Date 1917	Hour	Summary of Events and Information	Remarks and references to Appendices
Renghurst	Jan 2.		Opened Armoured Gun Boat Repair Shop in Regt Sects. Personnel to repair and re-issuing of Lewis Guns Belts. No men instruction.	
"	"	4	1000 Lewis Gun Belts converted with Cords attached completed by Divisional Labour and issued to Infantry Battalions in exchange for Canvas Belts.	
"	"	5.	Opened Gun Boat Repair Shop in Left Sect.	
"	"	6	18 Pdr Gun received for 241st Battery, to replace casualty.	
"	"	10	Vickers Machine Gun received for 147 Machine Gun Coy.	
"	"	11	One Lewis Gun received for 20th London Regiment.	

WAR DIARY

INTELLIGENCE SUMMARY.

(Erase heading not required.)

Army Form C. 2118.

Place	Date	Hour	Summary of Events and Information	Remarks and references to Appendices
Reninghelst	Jan 15		White Snow Sheets to cover Guns on snow covered ground issued to Divisional Artillery and reserve to all Artillery Units — one per Gun.	
	"	15	80 White Paticos Suits made in Divisional Shop & issued to Brigades in turn. 80 additional suits made and issued.	
	"	16		
	"	17	One Lewis Gun received for 15th London Regiment.	
	"	21	Changes in Divisional Artillery reorganisation. 104th Brigade attached to the Division & 235/6/8 Bgds reorganised. Reserve ammunition cancelled and Batteries of Brigade.	

Army Form C. 2118.

WAR DIARY
INTELLIGENCE SUMMARY.
(Erase heading not required.)

Instructions regarding War Diaries and Intelligence Summaries are contained in F. S. Regs., Part II. and the Staff Manual respectively. Title pages will be prepared in manuscript.

Place	Date	Hour	Summary of Events and Information	Remarks and references to Appendices
Roughton	Jan 27		25 ft Periscopes made & Div Armourer Shop rendered useful to G.O.C.	
"	"		Gun Box Repair Shop opened at Ordnance Dep't & Guns	
"	"		One Lewis received for 8th London Regiment	
"	28		with Gun Sheets made in Div Tailors Shop for Corps Artillery — made instructions A.D.O.S. 1 Corps.	
"	"		Additional 1000 Ground Sheets with Collars and Straps attached made by Div Tailors and issued.	
"	31		Latrine covers erected during the month and special cases of sickness among men of D.H.Q. Ordnance detachment non existent.	

18/2/17

A.J. Shrand
Capt. D.A.O.S. 47th Division
B.E.F.

2353 Wt. W2544/1454 700,000 5/15 D. D. & L. A.D.S.S./Forms/C. 2118.

No 152
Army Form C. 2118.

DADOS
47th London Division

Vol 2 3

WAR DIARY

INTELLIGENCE SUMMARY.

(Erase heading not required.)

Place	Date	Hour	Summary of Events and Information	Remarks and references to Appendices
Renninghelst	February 1917 Feb 8		100 White Patrol Suits (Coat and Trousers) for use on snow covered ground made in Div. Tailors Shop and issued to Infantry Brigades.	
	"	10	24 Lewis Guns received and issued to Infantry Battalions at the rate of 2 per Battalion each Battalion now in possession of 14 Lewis Guns. Bulk indents for the Pistols and Equipment required to complete to the scale sent to Base.	
	"	11	Further 100 White Patrol Suits made in Div. Tailors Shop and issued to Infantry Brigades.	
	"	15	Food container of special size and in accordance with D.H.Q. instructions made in Div. Armourers Shop, and sent for approval to Head Quarters.	

153

Army Form C. 2118.

WAR DIARY
INTELLIGENCE SUMMARY

(Erase heading not required.)

Place	Date	Hour	Summary of Events and Information	Remarks and references to Appendices
Renninghelst	Feb. 18		500 Ground Sheets with collar and flap attachment made in Div. Tailors Shop and issued to Infantry Battalions in exchange for ordinary ground sheets.	
"	19		1 4.5 Howitzer and Carriage received for D/104 Battery. These restrictions imposed. Lorries not used except in urgent cases and under D.H.Q. instructions	
"	22		1 18 pdr Gun and Carriage received for B/104 Battery.	
"	23		Part of Divisional Reserve of S.D. Clothing received, approximately 1800 Suits. Drawn under authority Q.M.G. 4/12 Q.A.3 9/2/17.	
"	25		Further 200 Ground Sheets with collar and flap attachment made in Div. Tailors Shop and issued to Infantry Battalions in exchange for ordinary ground sheets.	

Army Form C. 2118. /54

WAR DIARY
or
INTELLIGENCE SUMMARY.
(Erase heading not required.)

Place	Date	Hour	Summary of Events and Information	Remarks and references to Appendices
Renninghelst	Feb 26		1 Lewis Gun accessories for 8th Batt. London Regt.	
"	28		D.D.O.S. Second Army inspected Stores, Billets and Office. Captain Shead proceeded on leave.	

J.R. Smith
Lieut
A/DADOS
47th Division, B.E.F.

6/3/17.

Confidential

WAR DIARY
or
INTELLIGENCE SUMMARY.
(Erase heading not required.)

Army Form C. 2118.

D.A.D.O.S.
47th Division
Capt A. T. Skead

Nov 24

Place	Date	Hour	Summary of Events and Information	Remarks and references to Appendices
Renighest.	Nov 2		One Vickers Gun received for 141 Machine Gun Co.	
"	" 5		One 18 pdr Gun received for A 236 Battery. R.F.A.	
"	" 7		One 18 pdr Gun " " B 104 " "	
"	" 9		Two Lewis Guns received for 7th Battn.	
"	"	0934. Pte. F. Walters evacuated to Hospital with broken leg.		
"	" 10		D.A.D.O.S. returned from leave	
"	" 12		One 18 pdr Gun received for A 236 Battery. R.F.A.	

Army Form C. 2118.

WAR DIARY
or
INTELLIGENCE SUMMARY.
(Erase heading not required.)

Place	Date	Hour	Summary of Events and Information	Remarks and references to Appendices
Reninghelst	Mar 12		Instructions received from D.O.S. that Grants for R.A. Units and T.M. Batteries for Stores in Section 14 to 18 to the east in future to know Bdes. Units instructed to submit demands for these stores separately.	
"	"	14	104 Bde. R.F.A. (Army Artillery) transferred for Ordnance administration to O/C X Corps Troops. Outstanding demands forwarded vide instruction D.D.O.S. Second Army.	
"	"	"	One Lewis Gun received for 17th London Regt.	
"	"	17	6620 A/Cpl Crews. G.P. Bowmaker left for duty with D.D.O.S. Second Army	
"	"	19	568 Army Troops Co. R.E attached for Ordnance Services	

Army Form C. 2118.

WAR DIARY
or
INTELLIGENCE SUMMARY.
(Erase heading not required.)

Place	Date	Hour	Summary of Events and Information	Remarks and references to Appendices
Rennyhill	Jan 21		One Lewis Gun received for 7th Lincoln Regt	
"	"		Six Haversacks for Lewis Guns withdrawn from each Infantry Battn and returned to Base. Instructions QMG GHQ 1538/1/17/QA 3) 25/12/16.	
"	"	23	2nd Middlesex Labour Battn attached for Ordnance services.	
"	"	25	24 Lewis Guns received and issued to 12 Infy Battns viz. Two per Battn. Each Battalion now in possession of 16 Guns. Revolvers and Equipment to complete to this scale demanded from Base.	
"	"	"	5755 A/SergtCondr J.B.Clarke arrives for duty and attached 142 Brigade.	
"	"	"	183 Tunnelling Co. R.E attached for Ordnance Services.	

WAR DIARY
or
INTELLIGENCE SUMMARY.

Place	Date	Hour	Summary of Events and Information	Remarks and references to Appendices
Renighelst	Mar 26		142 Infantry Brigade left Divisional area. Lorries sent to Rear Rejoining Point.	
"	"		2nd Field Ambulance left Divisional Hd. Departure reported and outstanding demands forwarded to O.O. X Corps Troops.	
"	"		0 3399 L/Sgt. G. Whiting arrives for instruction in duties of Brigade Warrant Officer. A.O.C.	
"	28		1 Carriage Q.F. 18 pr received for A 235 Battery. R.F.A.	
"	"		5397 S.Q.M.S. N. La Patourel arrives for duty attached 141 Brigade Warrant Officer. A.O.C.	
"	30		One heavy Gun received for 15th London Regiment.	

Army Form C. 2118.

WAR DIARY
or
INTELLIGENCE SUMMARY.
(Erase heading not required.)

Place	Date	Hour	Summary of Events and Information	Remarks and references to Appendices
Reninghelst	Jan 31.		1000 Caps (converted Gorn Sheets) made in Tailors Shop during month and issued to Units in exchange for ordinary Ground Sheets.	
"	"		300 Fire Buckets made in Divisional Armourers Shop during month and issued to Camps in Area.	

A.J. Skead
Captⁿ D.A.D.O.S.
47th [London] Division
B.E.F.

3.2.17.

Army Form C. 2118.

WAR DIARY
or
INTELLIGENCE SUMMARY.
(Erase heading not required.)

Confidential
D.A.D.O.S.
47th Division
Capt. A. T. Shead

APRIL

Place	Date	Hour	Summary of Events and Information	Remarks and references to Appendices
1917 Remy belt	April 6th	1st	600 Lewis Gun covers for 7th London Regt.	VM 25
"		4	600 Lewis Gun covers received for 23 London Regt.	
"		5	25 Red Flags made in Divn Tailors Shop and issued to 142nd Brigade for training operations	
"		"	74 Waterproof Rations Bags made in Divn Tailors shop and issued to three Brigades in line.	
"		7	4500 Capes lined 150 received and available for use	
"		10	300 Royal West Surrey letter G attached for Ordnance Installation	

Army Form C. 2118.

WAR DIARY
or
INTELLIGENCE SUMMARY.

(Erase heading not required.)

Instructions regarding War Diaries and Intelligence Summaries are contained in F. S. Regs., Part II. and the Staff Manual respectively. Title pages will be prepared in manuscript.

Place	Date	Hour	Summary of Events and Information	Remarks and references to Appendices
Lenningfeld	Apr 11.		One 3" Stokes Mortar received for 141 T.M. Battery	
"	"		One Vickers Gun for 140 Machine Gun Company	
"	12		Lieut. W.B. Bannana arrives for instructions and duties for S.A.O.S.	
"	13		Two Vickers Guns received for 142 Machine Gun Co.	
"	"		One 2" Trench Mortar received for "Y" T.M. Battery	
"	16		One 6" Trench Mortar received for "Z" T.M. Batty	
"	18		Sho sent totches at Hoppenbrockschlag for issue of Winter Clothing. N.C.O. A.O.O. in charge.	

Place	Date	Hour	Summary of Events and Information	Remarks and references to Appendices
Remy Huts Camp	Apr 18	9000	Field Kits & mats Chair Maps returned and were 3000 to each Brigade mans D.A.Q. returned.	
"	23		One 18 Pdr Gun received f/p 536 Battery	
"	23		Sgt Canadian Railway Troops and 340 Rank Candians Coy attached for Ordnance References(?)	
"	24		Lieut W.B. Bourdeau attached to 39th Division for temp duty in absence of D.A.D.O.S. 39th Divn.	
"	"		Instructions for distributing straps to be worn by Infantry Runners, Signallers, Officers of Parties & c. issued to three Infantry Brigades	

Army Form C. 2118.

WAR DIARY
or
INTELLIGENCE SUMMARY.
(Erase heading not required.)

Instructions regarding War Diaries and Intelligence Summaries are contained in F. S. Regs., Part II. and the Staff Manual respectively. Title pages will be prepared in manuscript.

Place	Date	Hour	Summary of Events and Information	Remarks and references to Appendices
Longfossé	Nov 30.		Asking D.O.S. for extra drafts enquiry has been made in Dist. Remount Depôt sent to D.H.Q. for inspection.	
			2000 Grams Glucerine Collas sent this afternoon made in Dist. Indus. Dept. during the past few weeks to various Infantry Units in search for enemy Snow sleds.	

J. Head
Capt
A.D.V.S.
47th Division
B.E.F.

3/5/17.

Army Form C. 2118.

WAR DIARY
or
INTELLIGENCE SUMMARY.

(Erase heading not required.)

Confidential

D.A.D.O.S.
17th DIVISION.

Capt. A.T. SHEAD

Vol 26

Place	Date	Hour	Summary of Events and Information	Remarks and references to Appendices
RENINGHELST	MAY 2.		One Vickers Gun received for 140 Machine Gun Coy.	
"	3.		One Lewis Gun received for 21st Lancs Regt.	
"	5.		30,000 Box Respirator Pieces for Box Respirators received an consignments.	
"	5.		D.A.D.O.S. visits Calonne Base, A.D.O.S. X Corps, and Army.	
"	6.		One Lewis Gun received for 15 Lancs Regt.	
"	9.		2 Vickers Guns received for 143 Machine Gun Coy.	
"	11.		1500 Box Respirators received and issued to Units new D.H.Q. instructions.	

Army Form C. 2118.

WAR DIARY
or
INTELLIGENCE SUMMARY.
(Erase heading not required.)

Instructions regarding War Diaries and Intelligence Summaries are contained in F.S. Regs., Part II. and the Staff Manual respectively. Title pages will be prepared in manuscript.

Place	Date	Hour	Summary of Events and Information	Remarks and references to Appendices
Rangoon	May 13		1 Vickers Gun received for 142 Machine Gun Coy	
"	" 14		140 Infantry Brigade proceeds to Birmingham by train. Other Vickers Guns received for 32 Lewis Regt.	
"	"		Large consignment of Camp Equipment received for issuing under X Corps instructions	
"	"		One Vickers Gun received for 141 Machine Gun Coy	
"	16		Office Stores & Staff Car moved to GG23.C.9.4. Ondulow	
Ondulow	"		Lying at Rathenow	

Army Form C. 2118.

WAR DIARY
or
INTELLIGENCE SUMMARY.
(Erase heading not required.)

Place	Date	Hour	Summary of Events and Information	Remarks and references to Appendices
OUDERDOM	May 18		D.A.D.O.S. visits 140 Brigade Transport lines and also Battalions &c.	
"	19		400 Mags pads and Jaeger slips were issued to 140 Bde for Trench Stores.	
"	21		Attached tradesmen Tailors & Cooks attached 5th Field Ambulance for Inspection.	
"		11 AM	Battn Sergt Lance Regt attached for Ordnance Duties.	
"	23		Gun 18 pdr Carriage received for A 235 Battery.	
"	26	9.50	Body of unknown Tank full kit/equipment received from D.H.Q. and passed under Town Guide.	

Army Form C. 2118.

WAR DIARY
or
INTELLIGENCE SUMMARY.
(Erase heading not required.)

Place	Date	Hour	Summary of Events and Information	Remarks and references to Appendices
Ordnance			Large consignment of special stores packed ready for transfer with Ashard Divisional Ammunition Columns etc. remainders issued to Battalion.	
"	27		Charge of Brass Fuse Covers to Calais for Harley own Fuzes, Instructions, Instrn. 18 Hinere 185	
"	27		One Vickers Gun received for 142 Machine Gun Coy.	
"	28		Vickers Mg Gun Park Opened Ammunition etc received for 141 Machine Gun Coy	
"	30		One 18 pdr Gun received for B 235 Battery	
"	31		One Carriage 4.5 received for D 236 Battery	

3/6/17

F.J. Shaw
Capt. D.A.D.O.S
47th Division

Army Form C. 2118.

WAR DIARY
or
INTELLIGENCE SUMMARY.
(Erase heading not required.)

Copanhis D.A.D.O.S. 47th Division

JUNE Captain Shea Vol 27

Place	Date	Hour	Summary of Events and Information	Remarks and references to Appendices
Oudezeem G.23.C.9.4.	1917 June 3.		One 18 pdr Gun & Carriage recover'd for B/235 Battery.	
"	4		Camp Shewn between 1 A.M. and 2 A.M.	
"	"		One 18 pdr Gun recover'd for B/235 Battery.	
"	5		Two Vickers Guns rec'd for 142 machine Gun Coy. One 18 pdr Gun & Carriage rec'd for C/236 Battery.	
"	8		Two 4.5 How's & Carriage rec'd for D 236 Battery	
"	"		Camp Shewn 11pm to 2 A.M. One Lewis Gun recover'd for 20th London Regiment.	
"	9		One 18 pdr Carriage rec'd for C/236 Battery.	

Army Form C. 2118.

WAR DIARY
or
INTELLIGENCE SUMMARY.
(Erase heading not required.)

Instructions regarding War Diaries and Intelligence Summaries are contained in F.S. Regs., Part II and the Staff Manual respectively. Title pages will be prepared in manuscript.

Place	Date	Hour	Summary of Events and Information	Remarks and references to Appendices
Oudezeele. B.23.c.9.4.	9/5		Two Vickers Guns recd for 140. M.G.C.	
	"		One 18 pdr Gun & Carriage for A/236 Batty	
	"		Five Lewis Guns for 9th London Regt.	
	"		One do do do	
	10		One Vickers Gun recd for 140. M.G.C.	
	"		One 18 pdr Gun recd for A/235 Batty	
	"		One Gun & Carriage for C/236 Batty	
	"		One Lewis Gun recd for 18th Lon Regt	
	11		One Carriage & two 18 pdrs for B/236 Batty	
	"		Vickers Gun for 140. M.G.C.	
	"		do do do 142 do	
	"		2 Lewis Guns for 8th London Regiment.	

WAR DIARY or INTELLIGENCE SUMMARY

Army Form C. 2118.

Place	Date	Hour	Summary of Events and Information	Remarks and references to Appendices
WESTOUTRE	June 13		Office Depot & workshops moved from G.23.C.9.4. to Hostortre.	
"	"		One 18 pdr Gun returned for B 235 Batty	
"	14		Several Lewis Guns & I vickers rotation captured by 23rd and 24th London Regiments despatched to Base. Units re-equipped with clothing & Lewis Kit gun on return from trenches.	
"			One Lewis Gun for 23rd London Regt.	
"			Two " " 6th Lon Regt.	
"			Two " " 22nd London Regt.	
"			Two " " 2nd London Regt.	
"			One " " 18th do do	
"	16		D.16.9. and Inf Battns moved to Rest Area Blaringhem. Refitting by Armyff.	

Army Form C. 2118.

WAR DIARY
or
INTELLIGENCE SUMMARY.
(Erase heading not required.)

Instructions regarding War Diaries and Intelligence Summaries are contained in F.S. Regs., Part II. and the Staff Manual respectively. Title pages will be prepared in manuscript.

Place	Date	Hour	Summary of Events and Information	Remarks and references to Appendices
WESTOUTRE				
June	16		Rathen Oredaux heavy shelled at time of Regury. Stores received to complete A.O.C. One Carriage field 18pr received for A/236 Battery.	
"	18		Reinforcements to Essinghem. Filling Stores belt cartridges by Convoy.	
"	20		One 3" Trench Mortar for Z } I.R. Battery. " " " Y } do X One Lewis Gun received for 18th Lond Regt.	
"	21		One Lewis Gun for 6th Lond Regt.	
"	22		Visits air Bryan Scanymetor	
"	"		2 Vickers Guns for 141. M.G.C.	

Army Form C. 2118.

WAR DIARY
or
INTELLIGENCE SUMMARY.
(Erase heading not required.)

Place	Date	Hour	Summary of Events and Information	Remarks and references to Appendices
Westoutre	June 30		576 Q of Infantry Battn returns forwarded.	
"	"	"	Railway Returns forwarded.	

3/7/17

A.J. Wear
Capt
47th Division

Army Form C. 2118.

WAR DIARY
or
INTELLIGENCE SUMMARY.
(Erase heading not required.)

Confidential

D.A.D.S.
47th Division.
JULY.

Capt. A.J. Shead & Lieut. A.J. Dodds

Vol 28

Place	Date 1917.	Hour	Summary of Events and Information	Remarks and references to Appendices
WESTOUTRE	JULY. 1st.		1st. Canadian Tunnelling Coy. transferred from 41st. Division for administration.	
	3rd.		10th Railway Coy. R.E. " " " " " "	
	"		175th. Tunnelling Coy. R.E. " " " " " "	
	4th.		No. 5304. A/s. Condr. W.F. Aylett. A.O.C. returned to duty from leave.	
	5th.		Details 1st. Canadian Reserve Park transferred from 41st. Division.	
	6th.		94th Labour Coy. and 193rd. Labour Coy. " " " "	
	11th.		46th Labour Coy. transferred from II Anzac Corps Troops.	
	"		10th and 11th Australian F.A. Brigades. HQrs 1st. 2nd. + 3rd Sections. Aus. D.A.C. and HQrs. 4th. Aus. Div. Artillery transferred from 4th Australian Division.	
	13th.		Lieut. A.J. Bodds. A.O.D. arrived from A.D.O.S. X Corps. for temporary duty.	
	"		14th Coy. 4th Aus. Div. Train. A.S.C. transferred from 4th Aus. Division.	
	"		87th Labour Coy. transferred from II Anzac Corps Troops.	
	14th.		No. 3806. Condr. E.W. Buffee. A.O.C. awarded Silver Medal for long service + good conduct. (vide Corps Order 408 7/7/17.)	
	15th.		One Lewis Machine Gun received for 7th London Regt.	
	16th.		One " " " " 20th London Regt.	
	18th.		HQrs + No. 3. Sec. 4th Aus. D.A.C. transferred to 4th Aus. Divn.	

Army Form C. 2118.

WAR DIARY
or
INTELLIGENCE SUMMARY.
(Erase heading not required.)

Instructions regarding War Diaries and Intelligence Summaries are contained in F.S. Regs., Part II. and the Staff Manual respectively. Title pages will be prepared in manuscript.

Place	Date	Hour	Summary of Events and Information	Remarks and references to Appendices
WESTOUTRE	1917. JULY 18th		239th Machine Gun Coy. arrived from England and attached to HQrs. 47th Division.	
	19th		One Lewis Machine Gun received for 6th London Regt.	
			One " " " " 8th London Regt.	
	20th		Visited Railhead and Refilling points, also inspected Stores at Divl. Salvage Dump.	
	22nd		Capt. A.T. Shead. A.O.D. 47th Division proceeded to England on one month's special leave and handed over his duties temporarily to Lieut. A.T. Dodds. A.O.D.	
	24th		A/Cpl. J. Hynd. A.O.C. proceeded on 10 days special leave.	
			One Lewis Machine Gun received for 19th London Regt.	
			319th Road Construction Coy. transferred from II Anzac Corps Troops.	
	25th		1 Carriage 18 Pdr. received for C.B.4y. 236. Brigade. R.F.A.	
BERTHEN. R.21.d.5.2.	26th		Moved office and stores from Westoutre to Berthen.	
			4th Australian Divl. Artillery transferred to 41st Divn.	
			One Vickers Machine Gun received for 140th Machine Gun Coy.	
			One Lewis " " " 7th London Regt.	
	28th		Two 3" Stokes Trench Mortar Barrels received for 141st French Mortar Battery.	
			1st Canadian Tunnelling Coy; 1st Cav. Reserve Park., 175th Tunnelling Coy; 10th Railway Construction Coy. and	

Army Form C. 2118.

Instructions regarding War Diaries and Intelligence Summaries are contained in F. S. Regs., Part II and the Staff Manual respectively. Title pages will be prepared in manuscript.

WAR DIARY
or
INTELLIGENCE SUMMARY

(Erase heading not required.)

Place	Date 1917.	Hour	Summary of Events and Information	Remarks and references to Appendices
BERTHEN	JULY. 28th		and 46th. 87th. 94th. 136th. 193rd Labour Coys transferred to 41st. Division. No. 01247B. Sergt. J. Evans. A.O.C. transferred to A.D.O.S. X Corps for duty.	
			The work of equipping all units in the Division with the corrected ground sheet with collar and flap attachment is still proceeding. Divisional Tailors shop, and approximately 75% of the Division have now been supplied with these corrected sheets.	

Dated 1st August 1917.

A.J. Dodds. Lieut. AOS.
for D.A.D.O.S.
47th Division.

Army Form C. 2118.

WAR DIARY
or
INTELLIGENCE SUMMARY.
(Erase heading not required.)

DADS 47th Division
Copy in ink
Capt A.T. Skew

Vol 29

Place	Date	Hour	Summary of Events and Information	Remarks and references to Appendices
1917				
Bedford Ings	Aug 2		One 18 Pdr Gun procured for B/236 Battery, R.F.A.	
"	" 3	0/1803	Pk. A. Smith, A.O.C. arrives from Calais for duty.	
"	" 5		One 18 pdr Carriage received for C/236 Battery.	
"	" 6		Officer Stores and Gun Stores moved to W/Guides.	
Wizernes	" 10		One Anco QF 15 pdr for A/235 Battery, R.F.A. Received at Canal.	
"	" 12		1 Canadian Labor Battn and 111th Labr Co transferred to Asst Dir for Ordnance Services.	
"	" 13		340 Road Construction Coy to 2nd Corps Troops for ammunitions	
"	" 14		One 18 pdr Gun for B/235 U Battery R.F.A.	
"	" 17		Officer Stores and W/Guides reform to Ordnance Shed	
			20.G. 14.d.Central.	
	" 18		Transfer to II Corps Sgt. Army Lends for Gun Stores to Fifth Army Gun Park.	
28 G. 14 B.	" 21		Officer Stores and W/Guides known to Ordnance Shed 28 G.29.B.&.4.	

WAR DIARY
or
INTELLIGENCE SUMMARY.
(Erase heading not required.)

Army Form C. 2118.

Place	Date	Hour	Summary of Events and Information	Remarks and references to Appendices
Oudezem	Aug 21		The following Units transferred from 8th Division for annual tale by the 16th Div arty, HQrs 32, 33, 36, 55 Batty, 33rd F.A. Bde. HQrs 1,3,5 and 57 Batty, 45th F.A. Bde. X.Y.Z. 8th T.M. Batty W/8, H.T.M.B, HQrs 1,2 & 3 Sections 8th D.A.C.	
"	24		Capt A.H. Sheean D.A.D.O.S returned from leave	
"	25		Two Vickers Guns received for 142 M.G.C.	
"			" " " " " 239 M.G.C.	
"	26		Lieut. A Dodds to O.O.II Corps Troops for duty	
"	26		5. D.S.O. and 15th A.S.P. transferred to the following from X Corps Troops	
"	28		One 18 pdr Gun recd for 33rd Batty, R.F.A. 8th Divn.	
"	31		One Lewis Gun received for 22nd Lan B Regt	

Army Form C. 2118.

Instructions regarding War Diaries and Intelligence
Summaries are contained in F. S. Regs., Part II
and the Staff Manual respectively. Title pages
will be prepared in manuscript.

WAR DIARY
or
INTELLIGENCE SUMMARY.

(Erase heading not required.)

Place	Date	Hour	Summary of Events and Information	Remarks and references to Appendices
Ondurdorp	Aug 31		The following units attached to me for administration from date:- HQs 58. Dn. Artly, HQ & A.B.C.D Batlys 290 Bde. R.F.A, HQ's A.B.C.D Batlys 291st Bde. R.F.A. X Y Z / 58 T.M.B.'s V / 58 H.T.M. Bty 1,2 & 3 Sections 58th D.A.C. HQs Coy 58th A.S.C.	

September 2nd 1917.

Herbert
Capt. D.A.D.O.S.
47th Division

Army Form C. 2118

WAR DIARY
or
INTELLIGENCE SUMMARY
(Erase heading not required.)

2 A.D.S.S.
47th Division
Capt A.F. Shaw
Vol 30

Place	Date	Hour	Summary of Events and Information	Remarks and references to Appendices
Oudurdom			Confidential	
Sept	1st		The following Units to me for transmittals from 58th Divn:- HQ 58th RFA, HQ A,B,C,D 290 Brigade R.F.A, HQ A,B,C,D 291 Bde R.F.A, V, X, Y + Z M. Battys. H.Q, 1, 2 ,3 Secs D.A.C, H.Q, Coy Trains A.S.C.	
"	3		Units of 58th Division transferred to 58th Divn for trans=	
"	4		transfers to Second Army, Fifth Army Gun Parks cancelled and now outstanding on Fifth Army Gun Parks cancelled and no demands to be called.	
"	7		2 Lewis Guns received for 17th London Regt.	
"	9		1 Lewis Gun received for 32nd London Regt.	
"	13		2 Carriages 4.5 How received for D.235 Bde	
"	17		One Order 18 pdr received for B.236 B.Gy.	
"	19		Horse Officer, Stores and Workshops to Gouvernecourt	

Army Form C. 2118

WAR DIARY
or
INTELLIGENCE SUMMARY
(Erase heading not required.)

Instructions regarding War Diaries and Intelligence Summaries are contained in F. S. Regs., Part II. and the Staff Manual respectively. Title Pages will be prepared in manuscript.

Place	Date	Hour	Summary of Events and Information	Remarks and references to Appendices
Goeuvrecourt.	Sept 21st		47th Div HQ and 1 Coy Lewis to IX Corps troops, One W/O and two other Ranks LH attended	
"	23		Officers and Workshops moved to St Catherine.	
			Remained to first hug XIII Corps.	
			Rathuen Escuire.	
St Catherine	24.		Stores now received from Heavy Rovers, Calais and First Army Gun Parks.	
"	27.		One 18 pdr Gun and Carriage rec'd fr O235 Bde.	
"	28.		1 Lewis Gun rec'd for 17th Lon Regt.	
"			3 " " 5 " " 19th do	
"	29		1 Lewis Gun received for 7 London Regt.	

3/10/17

Allen
Capt
DADOS
47th (London) Division

WAR DIARY
or
INTELLIGENCE SUMMARY.
(Erase heading not required.)

Army Form C. 2118.

Confidential

D.A.D.S.
17th (London) Division
Capt A.T. Sloan

Vol 31

Place	Date	Hour	Summary of Events and Information	Remarks and references to Appendices
1917 St Catherine Oct		2	17th Div Adv Transport to one from IX Corps trops for ammunition	
"		3	Lorry and one M.B. of Two O.R. returns to duty	
"			Two 4.5 How's Carriages received for D235 Bty	
"		10	55th Labour Coy to	
"		13	One 3" T.M. received for 141. T.M.B.	
"			XIV Corps lorry's for ammunition	
"			One Vickers machine Gun received for 141. M.G.C.	
"		14	D.A.D.O.S. proceeded to Barcelona	
"			Standing duty for unit holding detachment	
"		16	One Lewis Guns for 2th London Regt	
"		18	One 3" T.M. received for 141. T.M.B.	
"		19	D.A.D.O.S. returns from Barcelona	
"			One Vickers gun for 140. M.G.C.	
"			One Lewis Gun made for 17th London Regt.	

A.T.Sloan
Capt D.A.D.O.S.
17th (London) Division

… WAR DIARY or INTELLIGENCE SUMMARY

Army Form C. 2118

D.A.D.O.S.
47th Divn
Capt. A. N. Sheat.

Vol 32

Place	Date	Hour	Summary of Events and Information	Remarks and references to Appendices
St Catherine	Nov 17		1 Vickers Gun demanded for 141 M.G.C.	
"	19		255 Vickers Gun Co joined Division.	
"	20		1 Vickers Gun received for 141 M.G.C. for units reserve nats.	
"	21		5th D.S.C. 25th Labour Group, 311 Road Constructn Coy, 149 Labour Co & 33 Ordnance workshop transferred new Corps instructions to 21 Divl Orders for authentication	
"	25		Moved to Achiet le Petit	
"	27		do do Hoplincourt	
"	29		do do Ruvelle	
"	30		Transferred to this Army IV Corps. Ammunition & Showmakers Shops arrived reserve from St Catherine	
"			5/15 Vickers Guns demanded by Vickers Guns Corps to replace others destroyed in Nov and receive tommy day 47th Divn	

A.N. Sheat
Capt. D.A.D.O.S.

3/12/17

WAR DIARY
or
INTELLIGENCE SUMMARY

Army Form C. 2118.

D.A.D.O.S.
47th (London) Division
Capt. A T SHEAD

Place	Date	Hour	Summary of Events and Information	Remarks
Neuville	1917 Dec. 1		Artillery units obtain urgent Lewis Gun Stores from advanced stores in charge of an N.C.O. at Havrincourt dump. To ensure necessary unserviceable parts produced and new issued in replacement.	
	4		1 Vickers Gun received for 140th Machine Gun Coy.	
	5		3 Lewis Guns received for 15th London Regt. 1 " " " B By. 285th Bde R.F.A. 1 18 Pdr Cover " " B By. 285th Bde R.F.A.	
			Moved Office to Ypres.	
Ypres	6		9 Lewis Guns received for 7th London Regt. 1 Vickers Gun " " 140th Machine Gun Coy.	
			20 Lewis Guns received for following units :- 17th London Regt 7, 18th London Regt 7, 20th Lon Regt 6.	
	8		5 Pnt Supply Col. from 31st Divn for administration by me. 2 Lewis Guns received for 23rd London Regt. H.Q. R.A., 62nd Div. t., H.Q. H.B.O+D Bys 310th & 312th Seige Bt An, H.Q. 3rd Trench Mortar Bde 62nd Div t., H.Q. 1, 2, 3 sAA Cos 62nd R.A.C. To 1 Cy 62nd Div t Train from 62nd Divt. to 47th Divt. for administration.	
	9		12 Lewis Guns received for 6th London Regt.	

Army Form C. 2118.

WAR DIARY
or
INTELLIGENCE SUMMARY.
(Erase heading not required.)

DADOS
47th Divn

M 33

Place	Date	Hour	Summary of Events and Information	Remarks and references to Appendices
1917 Ypres Area	10		1 Vickers Gun received for 140th Machine Gun Coy.	
	11		4 Lewis Guns received for following Units:- 23rd Lon Regt 1, 24th Lon Regt 1, 18th Lon Regt 2.	
			" " " 6th Lon Regt 5, 6th Lon Regt 2.	
			5 Vickers " " 142 M.G.Coy 3, 255th M.G.Coy 2.	
	12		1 Lewis Gun " 2/3rd London Regt	
	13		1 " " 24th " "	
	15		HQ. A, B, C, D Bys 310th Bde RFA to 59th Divn for administration	
			HQ. A, B, C, D Bys 312th Bde RFA, 30, Y, Z 147 [?] Motor Bys, HQ. 1st Bde Ses 62nd	
			Bde[?] HQ. Coy 62nd Divl Train to Lon Divs for administration	
	16		Office moved to Vlam[?]. Third Army. VIII Corps. Rochead, Albert.	
Neilly	20		4 Coys of 5th BSCC returned to unit. Service of 47th DSCC reported for duty.	
			Stores Shops moved to Halle from Neuville.	
	22		235th 236 Battle RFA, 47 NACC, X/47, Y/47, 47th 2M.Bys, HQ.Coy 47 Train, 1/2 Mob Vet	
			Section to 59th Divs for administration.	
	24		6th BSCC to 17th Bde & for administration 47th DSCC from 17th Divs to 47th Divs.	
	29		Capt A.J.Shead, DADOS proceeded on leave to England. Capt Smith Cont Gas Officer	
			acting DADOS.	

F.J.Skey Capt.
DADOS 47th (London) Division.

Army Form C. 2118.

Vol 34

WAR DIARY
or
INTELLIGENCE SUMMARY

(Erase heading not required.)

Confidential

D.A.D.O.S.
49th (Wyorks) Division
Capt. A.T. SHEAD.

Place	Date	Hour	Summary of Events and Information	Remarks and references to Appendices
Hilly	Jany 1		Third Army III Corps.	
			Ref tender to Corps if O.Rs entitled to Chevrons for service overseas.	
	3		Sgt. Dodds 1760 Y/C Div. Supply Shops granted leave to Paris.	
	5		All 49th Divl Ordnance units to one for administration from 59th Division	
			A/Capt. & A/D.A.D.O.S. J.B. Clarke A.O.D. appointed temporary D.O.S. for duration of absence	
	6		Offrs Stores & Shops moved to Ervillers fontenelle Third Army V Corps	
Ervillers			Fontenelle.	
			10.35.a.m. Comdg. Genl Staff Offr M.G.C. awarded Meritorious Service Medal.	
	7		JH.O. 1.O. & 200 dick 49th F.A.Col. to O.C. Third Army depot for administration	
	9		Batteries to indent direct for Gun spares during period R.A.O.D. in back area.	
	11		1 Store tent pitched at Pickford (Jacquigny) for use as store during shower precautions	
			& mobile fabrics are unable to be held.	
	12		1 Vickers Gun received for 142nd Machine Gun Coy.	
	13		100 pairs Gum Boots thigh received from I.O.M. Shops and issued to units	
	14		Sgt. Dodds returned from Paris.	
	15		Capt. A.B. Shead R.A.O.D. returned from leave.	

2353 Wt. W2514/1454 700,000 5/15 D. D. & L. A.D.S.S./Forms/C. 2118.

WAR DIARY
or
INTELLIGENCE SUMMARY.
(Erase heading not required.)

Army Form C. 2118.

Place	Date	Hour	Summary of Events and Information	Remarks and references to Appendices
Bhusawal	Jany 18		2000 pairs Gum Boots thigh received from V Corps dumps and issued to Units.	
	19		4 Cois A.C.C. serving with this Adoplacement entitled to Igm Bat. Riband demanded from Base.	
			3 Vickers Guns advised to 141? Machine Gun Coy.	
	21		10/8/23 RE Mobilization Stores left for unit with 1000 Ashich-le-Grand.	
	22		1/15 Bn. Piece reduced for a Coy 236ft Role R.F.A.	
	23		500 prefabricated Slabs (300 Long 3in Short) collected from V Corps dumps and issued to Units.	
Battlehead Camp	24		Men, Stores, & Shops moved to Battlehead Camp 1m 9 yds from Bhusawal.	
Thuis.	29		26 Anti-Aircraft Kits for Vickers Guns received from Ord. Cor. Ev. Coy to No 3.	
	30		18 Anti-Aircraft Mountings received for Vickers Hirse Guns.	
			9/7/23 RoI Mulgaon MO returned for duty from Ashich-le-Grand.	

1/2/18.

[signature]
Capt.

XXX1. 49th (Inday) Division

2353 Wt. W2544/1454 700,000 5/15 D. D. & L. A.D.S.S./Forms/C. 2118.

WAR DIARY
or
INTELLIGENCE SUMMARY.

Army Form C. 2118.

Vol 35

D.A.D.O.S. 47TH (LONDON) DIVISION.

Capt: A.T.S. HEAD.

Confidential

Place	Date	Hour	Summary of Events and Information	Remarks and references to Appendices
Titchfield Camp Fareham	1918 Feby 2		All Indents for 6th, 7th & 8th London Regts cancelled owing to these Units being disbanded. Infy. Bns now as follows:- 140 Bde. 15th, 17th & 21st London Regts. 141st Infy. Bde. 18th, 19th & 20th London Regts. 142nd Infy Bde. 22nd, 23rd & 24th London Regts.	
	6		1 x 18 Pdr piece received for B Bty 235th Bde R.F.A.	
			1 x 18 " " " " A " 236th " "	
			1 x 18 " " " " C " 236th " "	
	7/10		1 Lewis Gun received for 20th London Regt.	
			1 x 18 Pdr piece received for B Bty 236th Bde R.F.A.	
			1 x 18 " " " " B " 236th " "	
			1 x 4.5" How. " " " D " 235th " "	
	11		8 Lewis Guns received for Anti Aircraft purposes. One issued to each Battery R.F.A.	
	13		Pistols withdrawn from each M.T. Coy & A.S.C. Coy. and Rifles issued in replacement in accordance with G.R.O. 3292 of 1/2/16.	
	14		Capt A.T. Head A.O.D. D.A.D.O.S. proceeded to 70th Ordnance Depot for Ammunition Course.	
	15		1 Lewis Gun received for 15th London Regt.	
			2 Vicinam Machine Guns received and issued. One to 141st M.G. Coy & One to 255 M.G. Coy	

Army Form C. 2118.

WAR DIARY
or
INTELLIGENCE SUMMARY.

(Erase heading not required.)

Place	Date	Hour	Summary of Events and Information	Remarks and references to Appendices
[illegible] Camp. Ytres	Feby 16		18 Lewis Guns received for Anti-Aircraft purposes. Two issued to each Inf. Bn. Pistols Signal 1½" withdrawn from units and returned to Base.	
	19		1 × 4.5" How piece received for D Bty 236th Bde R.F.A.	
			1 × 18 Pdr " " B " 235th " "	
	22		3 Lewis Guns received for Anti-Aircraft purposes. One issued to each Field Coy R.E.	
	23		Office, Stores Workshops moved to Bus. Dump taken over from D.A.D.O.S. 17th Divn.	
Bus.	24		5 Hitchkiss Guns demobilised. One for each by ADC & one for 241st Employment Coy.	
	26		Reduction of Establishment of Divisional Workshop completed. Stores held at H.Q. Dump pending further instructions as to disposal.	
	28		26 Lewis Guns received for Anti-Aircraft purposes and issued as follows:- Each Inf. Bn. 2, each Battery R.F.A. 1.	
			11 Vickers Guns received for 141st Machine Gun Coy.	
			184 Sets Packsaddlery returned to O.O. Third Army Corps Nurlu	

1/3/18.

[signature] Capt
D.A.D.O.S. 47th (London) Division

WAR DIARY
INTELLIGENCE SUMMARY

Army Form C. 2118.

DADOS. 47th (London) Division. Capt. A.T. SHEAD

Place	Date 1918 March	Hour	Summary of Events and Information	Remarks
BUS.	1		4 Machine Gun Coys of this Division amalgamated and known as 47th Bnt Machine Gun Bn.	
	3		5 Hotchkiss Guns received for Anti-Aircraft purposes and issued 1 to 241st Bnt Employment Coy and 1 to each Coy of Dut. Train A.S.C.	
	6		Lewis and Vickers Guns of all units inspected by A.S.A.	
	9		1 x 15 Pdr Gun. Carr. Limber received from Gun Park and issued to Dut. Artillery for Anti-tank purposes.	
	10		Issues of Gun Stores to be ceased from Adv: Ord: Gun Park No 3 Bapaume. Indent to Gun Park No 3 Albert. Stores now delivered to Divisions and not collected as from Bapaume.	
	19		Q.M. Stores of 22nd London Regt at Rocquigny inspected by A.D.O.S. V Corps. Everything satisfactory.	
	21		Dump at Bus shelled at intervals.	
COMBLES	22		Officer, Stores, Shops moved to Combles. 5 light Railway trucks loaded with Ordnance Stores and sent with Convoy to rear for safety. All Stores cleared from Bus by 4:30 pm just before enemy entered village	

Army Form C. 2118.

WAR DIARY
or
INTELLIGENCE SUMMARY.
(Erase heading not required.)

Place	Date 1918 March	Hour	Summary of Events and Information	Remarks and references to Appendices
COMBLES	23		Dumps at Combles heavily shelled.	
ALBERT.	23		Moved to Albert. Unimportant Stores on Lorries sent to Base in truck from Albert Railhead. Albert heavily bombed during night 23-24th. 2 Lorry loads of S.A.A. collected and dumped at Contalmaison.	
ALBERT-AMIENS Rd nr RIBEMONT	24		Moved to Albert-Amiens Rd. nr Ribemont.	
WARLOY	25		Moved to Warloy. 1 Lorry sent to Albert to collect Rifles & did not return owing to breakdown and was abandoned near Albert - since recovered.	
VAUCHELLES	26		Moved to Vauchelles.	
PUCHVILLERS	27		Moved to Puchvillers. 46 Lewis Guns received & issued to Units	
RUBEMPRÉ	29		Moved to Rubempré 50 " " " "	
	30		42 Vickers Guns received & issued to Machine Gun Bn.	
	31		36 Lewis Guns received and issued to Units.	

1/4/18

Kerr
Capt.
D.A.D.O.S. 47th (London) Division

Army Form C. 2118.

WAR DIARY
or
INTELLIGENCE SUMMARY

L.A.S.O.S.
47th (Lon) Divion
47th (Lon) Divion. 236 Brigade Eng FA Stan

Vol 37

Place	Date	Hour	Summary of Events and Information	Remarks and references to Appendices
RUBEMPRÉ	1918. April 1		Four 3" trench mortars received for 141 T.M. Battery. H.Q, A, B, C, D Batty. 235 Brigade. H.Q, A, B, C, D Batty & 236 Brigade. 1 Coy 47th Div Train to 62 Divion for administration administered.	
	5		S.A.A. Section 47th D.A.C. to me for administration from 3rd Army Troops to 1.	
	6		6 Vickers Guns received for 47th M.G. Batts	
	8		Eight 3in T.M's received for 140 T.M. Battery " " " 142 do	
DOMART	12		Move to Domart.	
CANCHY	13		Move to Canchy. III Army X Corps. Railmen at Riquier.	

Army Form C. 2118.

WAR DIARY
or
INTELLIGENCE SUMMARY.
(Erase heading not required.)

Instructions regarding War Diaries and Intelligence Summaries are contained in F. S. Regs., Part II. and the Staff Manual respectively. Title pages will be prepared in manuscript.

Place	Date	Hour	Summary of Events and Information	Remarks and references to Appendices
CANCHY	1918 Sept 16		1,000 O.R. known not long to 63 Divn to administer the Divn in accordance with G.R.O. 3783	
	17		8 Lewis Guns received for units as follows:- 22 Regt 1, 23rd Regt 4, 4th R.W.F. 2, 23 Regt 1. 1 Vickers Gun received for M.G. Batn.	
	18		1 Lewis Gun received for 15th Lin. Regt. 10×6" Truds for his Decrim 5 cable for X & Y T.M. Batys.	
	25		4 rounds A.A.G.Supt A.A. spcial failure issued to M.G. Batn for test report.	
	26		36 Lewis Gun received and issued to various Bns.	
	30		Returns rendered.	
			H.G./P.S.	

Rivers
Capt. A/Q M(Cdy) Divn.

Army Form C. 2118.

Confidential

WAR DIARY
or
INTELLIGENCE SUMMARY.
(Erase heading not required.)

DADOS
47th (London) Divn

Vol 38

Instructions regarding War Diaries and Intelligence Summaries are contained in F.S. Regs., Part II. and the Staff Manual respectively. Title pages will be prepared in manuscript.

Place	Date	Hour	Summary of Events and Information	Remarks and references to Appendices
Cavilly	1st		Office Headquarters moved to Beaucourt	
to BEAUCOURT	2		Ludovic Dymant III Corps 4th Army.	
"	3		Lieut Linscham A.O.D. from 18th Divn V6 No Divions for duty	
"	9		03242/2 No. 1 Serm ADC to ADOS III Corps for duty	
"			5 Divns Divisions + to R.W.F. 1st Bn 22nd Regt	
"	10		235/236 Bdes R.F.A. Nos 1 & 2 Subs/47th DAC 101 Coy 47th Bn	
"			From us to our stances from 62nd Divn and from us to	
"			6.0 found any troops to.	
"	11		Money of Worthybrokparts by L.B.OS Fourth Army'	
"	12		ADOS III Corps V	
"	13		100 Sets of Packsaddles recieved from Brsio.	
"	15.		Travelle A.O.D. to L.& 12th Divisions for duty	
"	19.		Two 6" T.M's recd & issued 1 each to X & Y. T.M Bs.	
"	20		01467 4/c W. Ward to from G.Q. Found Army to us for duty	

2353 Wt. W2544/1454 700,000 5/15 D. D. & L. A.D.S.S./Forms/C. 2118.

Army Form C. 2118.

WAR DIARY
or
INTELLIGENCE SUMMARY.
(Erase heading not required.)

Instructions regarding War Diaries and Intelligence Summaries are contained in F. S. Regs., Part II. and the Staff Manual respectively. Title pages will be prepared in manuscript.

Place	Date	Hour	Summary of Events and Information	Remarks and references to Appendices
BEAUCOURT	1/5			
	23		HQ A B C D Btys 235 & 236 Bdes RFA HQ to 192 Subln 47th DAC to 1 Copy 47th Div Trains to me for amendments from OO. Point Map Tnefr. No 1.	
	25		1/36 Lewis Guns issued & orders given to each Inf Battn.	

Ackroyd
Major, RAOC.
47th Division

5/6/18

Army Form C. 2118.

WAR DIARY
or
INTELLIGENCE SUMMARY.
(Erase heading not required.)

D.A.D.O.S. 41st (Cavalry) Division

Vol 39

Instructions regarding War Diaries and Intelligence Summaries are contained in F. S. Regs., Part II. and the Staff Manual respectively. Title pages will be prepared in manuscript.

Confidential

Place	Date	Hour	Summary of Events and Information	Remarks and references to Appendices
BEAUCOURT	June 3		No 5/5755 S/Sergt A.S. Clarke A.O.C. admitted to Hospital	
	6		No 5/539 S/Sergt N.R. Laborel A.O.C. admitted to Hospital	
	8		Office Stores moved to T.27.D Central Sheet 57.D on account of hostile shelling	
	10		Lewis Gun Mountings made according to design for motor cars and inspected by D.A.C. Division	
	13		1 x 15 pdr piece received for A.B.+ 236th Bde R.F.A.	
	14		No 0/35513 Pte L. Hawkins A.O.C. observed furlough from France on nights of 14, 15, 16, 17, 18 days (including H.O.O.) Multiform A.O.C.	
	16		2 Vickers Guns received at 47th Machine Gun Bn	
	17		5/7123 Pte L. Mobligator H.C. proceeded to England on leave for fourteen days at home	
	18		3/4443 S/Sergt A. Gray A.O.C. arrived to do duty in relief of S/Sergt N.R. Laborel	
			15 pdr Shells & Cartridges moved to Cavillon - Pickes Bury Sta Somme	
CAVILLON	20			
	23		4 pairs No 16 binos & 5 Box II Solenoids from Eng Base Port by R.A.C. to replace war numbers Lost T pieces	
	26-30		12 Cases of R.V.O. on departmental during this period	

Signed...
Major
D.A.D.O.S. 41st (Cavalry) Division

2353 Wt. W3544/7454 700,000 5/15 D. D. & L. A.D.S.S./Forms/C. 2118.

10/7/18

MAJOR A.T. SHEAD
D.A.D.O.S.
47 L (London) Division.

VR 40

WAR DIARY
or
INTELLIGENCE SUMMARY.

Army Form C. 2118.

(Erase heading not required.)

Place	Date	Hour	Summary of Events and Information	Remarks and references to Appendices
CAVILLON	1918 Feb 1		1 Lewis Gun handed over to Windsor Regt.	
	3		Indented by A.D.O.S. Fourth Army.	
	4		Report received to A.A.& Q.M.G. 47 Divn. for information of Divnl Cmdt showing number of cases of Influenza including P.U.O. in Detachment and treated regimentally as '19.	
	5		No. 07400 S/ M/S W.H. King A.O.C. arrived for duty from No 1 Ord. Mob. Workshop in relief of No 21955 S/Cmd.³ G.R. Clarke	
	6		12 Lewis Guns received and issued to Infantry Bns to complete to Scale G.	
	7		1 Vickers Gun demanded from Gun Park for training purposes of Machine Gun Bn kept out of Gun.	
	8		Exchanger Rifle Grenade issued to Inf. Bns to complete to 96 per Bn.	
			No. 07400 S/ M/S W.H. King A.O.C. appointed a/S Cmd³	
	9		12 Lewis Guns received and issued 4 to each Lethal Coy R.E. Sleeping-Bag - design for connecting form R.E. Blanket for use in lieu of Blanket submitted to H.Q. 47ᵗʰ Divn.⁵ for consideration.	
	13		Office Forms, & Shops moved to Molliens-au-Bois. Faiload. Indanvelle.	

Army Form C. 2118.

WAR DIARY
or
INTELLIGENCE SUMMARY.
(Erase heading not required.)

Place	Date	Hour	Summary of Events and Information	Remarks and references to Appendices
CAVILLON	July 16		Major A.J. Sheat. D.A.D.O.S. proceeded on leave to England.	
	19		Depôt inspected by D.D.O.S. Fourth Army. & A.D.O.S. III Corps.	
	21		1 Vickers Gun received from Gun Park for Machine Gun Bn for training purposes.	
	25		16 Lewis Guns received for A.A. purposes and issued 2 each to Batteries R.F.A.	

7/8/18

Armstrong
Major
D.A.D.O.S. 47th (London) Division

Army Form C. 2118.

Confidential

WAR DIARY
or
INTELLIGENCE SUMMARY.
(Erase heading not required.)

D.A.D.O.S.
47th (LONDON) DIVISION
Major A.T. SHEAR

VOL 41

Place	Date 1918	Hour	Summary of Events and Information	Remarks and references to Appendices.
MOLLIENS-AU-BOIS	Aug 1		1×18 Pdr piece issued to A.Bty 236th Bde R.F.A.	
	2		1×18 Pdr Carriage issued to " " "	
	6		Depôt inspected by D.D.O.S. Fourth Army.	
	7		1×18 Pdr piece issued to B.Bty 235th Bde R.F.A.	
	9		Issue of Panoramascopes to 10th R.F.A completed.	
PONT NOYELLES	12		Office etc & Stores moved to Pont Noyelles. III Corps, Fourth Army.	
			1×4·5" How piece issued to 10 Bty 235th Bde R.F.A. Outrancourt.	
	18		Depôt inspected by A.D.O.S. III Corps.	
	19		1×4·5" How piece issued to B.Bty 236 Bde R.F.A.	
	20		1×4·5" " " " B.Bty 235th " "	
	22		6 Stokes Guns issued & received to 47th Machine Gun Bn.	
	23		6 " " " " " "	
			10 Lewis Guns received & issued as follows. 6 to 18 th Bn Lon. Regt, 3 to 19 th Bn Lon Regt, 1 to 20 th Bn Lon.	
	24		1×4·5" How piece & Carriage for B.Bty 235th Bde R.F.A.	

Army Form C. 2118.

WAR DIARY
or
INTELLIGENCE SUMMARY.
(Erase heading not required.)

Instructions regarding War Diaries and Intelligence Summaries are contained in F. S. Regs., Part II. and the Staff Manual respectively. Title pages will be prepared in manuscript.

Place	Date	Hour	Summary of Events and Information	Remarks and references to Appendices
PONT. NOYELLES	Aug. 24		24 Lewis Guns received & issued to 18th London Regt.	
			12 " " " " " 18th " "	
	25		1×18 Pr piece issued to C By 285 Bde R.F.A.	
			10 Lewis Guns received & issued to 19th London Regt.	
			12 " " " " " 1st " "	
			16 " " " " " 17th "	
HEILLY	26		6 Mtr Stores r/o/180h/56 issued to "Steffy"	
			1×18 Pr piece issued to A By 236 Bde R.F.A.	
			2 Vickers Guns received & issued to 47th Machine Gun Bn.	
			1×18 Pr piece issued to C By 235 1st Bde R.F.A.	
HIDDEN WOOD NAMETZ	30		Office & Stores moved to Mametz	

4/9/18

[signature]
Major
A.D.O.S. 47th Division

Army Form C. 2118.

WAR DIARY
or
INTELLIGENCE SUMMARY.
(Erase heading not required.)

D.A.D.O.S.
47th (London) DIVISION

MONS AT SHEAD. Vol 4 + 2

Instructions regarding War Diaries and Intelligence Summaries are contained in F. S. Regs., Part II. and the Staff Manual respectively. Title pages will be prepared in manuscript.

Place	Date	Hour	Summary of Events and Information	Remarks and references to Appendices
(Confidential)				
MAMETZ.	3		24 fuze Guns received, 12 for 15th Lon: Regt & 12 for 17th Lon Regt.	
	4		30 " " " 21 " 20th " & 9 " 21st "	
			1 × 18 Pdr Gun & Carr. received for A Bty 236th Bde R.F.A.	
MAUREPAS	6		Moved to Maurepas.	
ALLOUAGNE	9		Moved to Allouagne. Lyth Army, XIII Corps. Railhead Allouagne Siding	
	11		Depôt inspected by A.D.O.S. XIII Corps.	
	12		1 × 18 Pdr Carr. received for 16 Bty 236th Bde R.F.A.	
	15		37 fuze Guns received & issued 18 for 21st Lon Regt & 19 for 16th London Regt.	
			9 " " " " " " " " to 19th London Regt.	
			8 " " " " " " " " to 18th " "	
			1 × 18 Pdr piece issued to B.Bty 235th Bde R.F.A, 2 × 4.5" How guns received 1 to 19th Bty R.F.A.	
			1 to B/236th Bty R.F.A. 4 × 18 Pdr Carr. issued, 1 to B/235th Bty R.F.A, 1 to A/235th " "	
			2 " " " to A/236th Bty R.F.A. 1 × 18 Pdr Gun Carr. issued to C/236th Bty R.F.A.	
	18		1 × 18 Pdr piece issued to C/236th Bty R.F.A. 6 fuze guns issued 1 to 19th Lon Regt & 7 to 22nd Lon Regt.	
	21		First Blanket sun-now received for Division & issued.	
HAUTECLOQUE	29		Moved to Hautecloque	

4/10/18.
K. Ebery Major.
D.A.D.O.S. 47th (London) Division

Army Form C. 2118.

WAR DIARY
or
INTELLIGENCE SUMMARY.

Major A.T.S. Head M.C.
D.A.D.O.S. 47th DIVISION

Confidential

(Erase heading not required.)

Place	Date 1918 NOV	Hour	Summary of Events and Information	Remarks and references to Appendices
WILLEMS	1		Office Stores moved to Wattines From in Beraut (field).	
LA TOMBE	12		" " " " to Jambe (Jurnai)	
	15		Boot Shoes received from Base, Clothing, Boots, Caps, Haversacks the sent to Town Major Tournai for issue to returning Prisoners of War from Germany.	
OHERENG	17		Office Stores moved to Ohereng	
LONINGHEM	26		" " " " Loninghem	
AUMINASTIE	28		= Stores & Shops " " Aublaigne. Office remaining at Loninghem for administration of all troops in Div: Area. by me.	

1/12/18

[signature]
Major
D.A.D.O.S. 47th Division

Army Form C. 2118.

WAR DIARY
or
INTELLIGENCE SUMMARY.

(Erase heading not required.)

Confidential. MAJOR A.T. SHEAD. MC
DADOS 47th DIVISION

Instructions regarding War Diaries and Intelligence Summaries are contained in F. S. Regs., Part II and the Staff Manual respectively. Title pages will be prepared in manuscript.

Place	Date 1918 DEC	Hour	Summary of Events and Information	Remarks and references to Appendices
ALLOUAGNE	4		Orders received for change of Base to Havre from Calais and GHQ 0S 28/4.	
	5		Cancellation of 88 W/4 received. Continue to demand supplies from Calais.	
	8		Richonnah Station Billet Reps. despatched to Records to personnel of Regiment.	
	9		Third Ballot opened. Units authorized to submit Indents.	
	12		All demands on Gun Park cancelled. Indents estimated to Base for all Lorries outstanding.	
	14		Major Shead DADOS proceeded to England on 30 days Special Leave.	
	16		1/16 Major Tinker relieved him. Pr. I See 47th DAC.	
	17		Clothing Ren's difficult of Supt experienced. Report received to DNQ.	
	20		Shoemakers moved to Dunkel.	
	26		5 trucks of Blankets received from Base to complete Div't. to 3 per man.	
			Lieut Eut Booker RAOC ranked on relief of Major Shead.	

1/1/19

[signature] Major
DADOS 47th Division.

2353 Wt. W2544/1454 700,000 5/15 D.D. & L. A.D.S.S./Forms/C. 2118.

Nov to Jan 42

Army Form C. 2118.

MAJOR A.T. SHEAD. M.C.
DADOS
47th DIVISION

WO 45

WAR DIARY
or
INTELLIGENCE SUMMARY.
(Erase heading not required.)

Confidential

Instructions regarding War Diaries and Intelligence Summaries are contained in F. S. Regs., Part II and the Staff Manual respectively. Title pages will be prepared in manuscript.

Place	Date	Hour	Summary of Events and Information	Remarks and references to Appendices
AUCHEL	Jan 1			
	2		Great delay in arrival of trucks from Base experienced.	
	10		1 Corn 465 Shoes received for 189th 1895 & 272 Bde. Harness Saddlery being returned by units, rendered surplus by horses being sent away.	
	17		28 Rcts being issued it lieu of ankle boots, only sizes 8 & 9 of the latter available at Base.	
	21		No pair Gum Boots Short received and issued to Units of 47th Divt. Artillery.	
	24		1 Col. I. Synd RAOC demobilized in England, while on leave.	
	26		DADOS inspected eto for Dump near Rennes touched to employ with RAOC order 906 of 23/1/19.	

1/2/19

Nevins
Major
DADOS 47th Division

WAR DIARY
or
INTELLIGENCE SUMMARY

Confidential

Major A.T. SHEAD. M.C.
DADOS
47th DIV 15107

Vol 4

Place	Date	Hour	Summary of Events and Information	Remarks and references to Appendices
AUCHEL	Feb 1		Orders issued to units to return Watches, Compasses, Binoculars &c.	
	6		2/Lieut W.H. King RAOC proceeded to England on Demobilization	
	12		Cial shortage of Gunners' leather purchased by DADOS	
	14		S/L S. Parkin RAOC demobilized whilst in England on Leave.	
			3×4·5 How: guns received. 1 for 15 Bde, 189th A.F.A. Bde, & 1 for 10 Bde, 235th Bde R.F.A.	
	19		Instructions received allowing Rush demands. Two demands made.	
	25		Office Stores & Shops moved to Pernes. Office from Auykham (Bns) Shops from Auchel.	
PERNES	26		Major Shead. DG1904 returned from leave.	
	28		2/Lt Ed. Parker. RAOC proceeded to X Corps. Arrangements completed to Eng.! Bns. being demobilized under RAOC instructions	
			orders for release received from Corps, which instructed from this Office.	

1/3/19

[signature] Major
DADOS 47th Division

www.ingramcontent.com/pod-product-compliance
Lightning Source LLC
Chambersburg PA
CBHW082012220426
43670CB00014B/2609